ANNOTATED TEACHER'S

Social Studies
Reading Strategies

Program Consultant
Dr. Kate Kinsella
San Francisco State University
San Francisco, California

Globe
Fearon

Upper Saddle River, New Jersey
www.globefearon.com

Program Consultant

Dr. Kate Kinsella
Dept. of Secondary Education and
Step to College Program
San Francisco State University
San Francisco, CA

Consultant

John Edwin Cowen, Ed.D.
Assistant Professor, Education/Reading
Program Coordinator, Graduate M.A.T./
Elementary Education
School of Education
Fairleigh Dickinson University
Teaneck, NJ

Supervising Editor: Lynn W. Kloss
Senior Editor: Renée E. Beach
Editorial Assistant: Jennifer Watts
Writer: Sandra Widener
Production Editor: Laura Benford-Sullivan
Cover and Interior Design: Sharon Scannell
Electronic Page Production: Linda Bierniak, Phyllis Rosinsky
Manufacturing Supervisor: Mark Cirillo

Printed in the United States of America   2 3 4 5 6 7 8 9 10 04 03 02 01

ISBN: 0-130-23790-6

1-800-848-9500
www.globefearon.com

Contents

Foreword by Dr. Kate Kinsella

How does the reading task change as students move from elementary school to middle school?

In elementary classrooms, instruction is focused on helping students "learn to read." On the threshold of adolescence, students experience a quantum leap in moving from the carefully monitored narrative reading tasks of their elementary language arts instruction to the conceptually and linguistically dense texts they must independently navigate in their middle school coursework. Beyond fifth grade, students are routinely expected to not only tackle core works of literature, but also more frequently "read to learn" from expository texts that explain central lesson concepts and processes in diverse subject areas.

Classroom experience and educational research suggest most students have few effective strategies to apply to learning from expository texts. Middle school and high school students—whether high achieving or less prepared—need developmental content literacy instruction to extend and refine the reading and writing abilities they often bring from their elementary education.

How do you define "content literacy"?

McKenna and Robinson (1990) define content literacy as the ability to use reading and writing to acquire new content in a specific subject area. A student who is content literate has a heightened awareness and use of the structure and features of distinct informational texts, such as a newspaper article or a research report, and knows how to read in strategic ways to obtain knowledge from them. In addition, this text-wise reader makes a critical distinction between reading and analyzing an expository text in order to identify critical information to be learned, as opposed to later mastering the material by organizing it in some meaningful form of study notes.

In contrast, less sophisticated readers may possess considerable prior knowledge about the Civil War, yet lack the requisite literacy tools to confidently read and learn from a relevant textbook chapter or primary source document. They struggle to focus their attention appropriately and identify more significant information within a chapter section, often because they are unfamiliar with the function of organizational features such as an introduction, subheadings, topic sentences, and transitional expressions. Lacking this expository "text-wiseness," they tend to view all assigned reading as some form of "story," and predictably start at the chapter beginning, then progress slowly and aimlessly until they lose both stamina and motivation.

How can all teachers help expand students' content literacy?

Educators in every subject area should have as a primary instructional goal teaching students *how* to learn and not just *what* to learn. It is unrealistic and irresponsible to expect students in upper-elementary classrooms and beyond to adopt—through osmosis, incidental instruction, or voluntary pleasure reading—an informed and flexible approach to reading and learning from curricula in distinct fields of study. Young learners should not be abandoned to their own relatively unproductive devices to develop critical competencies for higher education and the challenging Information Age arena.

As interdisciplinary colleagues, we must therefore strive to move beyond the rhetoric of inclusive, multicultural education and explore collaboratively and comprehensively what is truly involved in educational access and equity. Teachers in reading classrooms and content classrooms alike can indeed make concrete strides in this direction by ensuring that all learners are granted challenging, yet accessible core reading currricula, as well as the cognitive secrets and strategies of content-literate students. By making explicit the potent strategies used by competent students to read, study, and learn across the subject areas, we will be able to successfully empower all students.

How can the Reading Strategies *series help students read to learn?*

The *Reading Strategies* series is an invaluable resource for teachers who have been searching for curricular guidance in crafting a dynamic course to prepare young readers for the literacy demands of content-area classrooms. Several features of this informational reading and study skills series make it a particularly appealing and pedagogically sound curriculum choice. The eclectic array of topical crosscurricular selections will be seen as an instructional boon to all teachers who have struggled in vain to compile a viable portfolio of engaging, clearly written, and unintimidating informational texts. Novice readers in the content areas benefit from sustained practice with relatively brief yet challenging expository selections, which pique their curiosity in the subject matter while providing a productive vehicle for strategy application. Less prepared students, who have habitually approached textbook assignments with trepidation, are in particular need of routine rather than periodic success with informational reading in all of the core subject areas.

This series further encourages reticent academic readers by introducing a manageable and developmentally appropriate tool kit of strategies for learning from informational texts. Unlike recreational narrative texts, informational text assignments typically require a more active and focused stance, multiple readings, and some form of synthesized notes for study and review. As students work through the book, they are exposed to an accessible repertoire of strategies for reading to learn, and given ample opportunities to apply each strategy to new literacy tasks.

The *Reading Strategies* series can serve as the vital curricular scaffold for a course focusing upon early content literacy development. However, this series requires teachers to become inspiring reading coaches who can provide a compelling rationale for each strategy, dynamic modeling, and abundant encouragement and praise at every stage.

About the *Reading Strategies* Series

The *Reading Strategies* series has been designed to teach students those strategies that will help them comprehend language arts material. The students who will most benefit from these books are students who may be able to understand individual words, but have difficulty assembling ideas into a meaningful whole.

Why Use Reading Strategies? The strategies taught in the Student Edition have been adapted and, in some cases, created, to solve problems students frequently have with reading comprehension. All have as their goal giving students tools they can use when they approach any reading assignment, especially the often-challenging material in content-area texts.

The Steps of the Strategies This four-step approach helps students become actively involved with their reading.

> **Step 1: Preview.** Students look over what they will read to create a context for learning and to focus their attention.
>
> **Step 2: Read.** Students read actively, thinking about what they know and looking for answers to questions they have generated.
>
> **Step 3: Take Notes.** Students take notes on what they have read, identifying major points and supporting details, and reflecting on what they have learned.
>
> **Step 4: Review.** Students review what they have read by writing a summary or practicing what they have learned in some other way.

The Student Edition The Student Edition provides the following:
- Students use a step-by-step process to learn the four strategies.
- Students apply the strategies to selections in a specific content area.
- Students learn skills for understanding words in context in Vocabulary Strategies, a vocabulary handbook.

Using the Student Edition The Student Edition supports students in learning to use reading strategies. Included are:
- Unit Openers that present the strategies students will find in each content area.
- Strategy Tips that make suggestions for using the strategy effectively.
- Graphic organizers that have student-created notes and space for students to add their own notes.
- Vocabulary Tips that offer clues for understanding the meaning of new words.
- Test Tips that help students understand how to answer test questions.
- Unit Reviews that can be used as informal reviews or as practice tests.
- Vocabulary Exercises that students can apply to all of their assignments.
- Additional readings at the end of the text that give students an opportunity for further review.
- A Strategy Quick Review that serves as a brief refresher.

Using this Annotated Teacher's Edition This Annotated Teacher's Edition reinforces the lessons in the Student Edition. Included are:
- Answers at point of use.
- Detailed Lesson Plans for teaching and modeling the strategy lessons.
- Lesson Notes for all the lessons in the Student Edition and the Vocabulary Strategies.
- Internet Connections to help students extend their knowledge of the topic.
- Reproducible Graphic Organizers to support all the strategies.

Teaching Reading to Learn

Teaching Tip

Choose a selection from your classroom text to use with the following techniques.

The following pages contain suggestions for teaching students how to read to learn. To apply any of the strategies introduced in the *Reading Strategies* series, students need to engage actively with text before, during, and after they read. Students should practice these behaviors until they become automatic. Because these behaviors are simply activities effective readers do without thinking, they can be taught successfully by both reading teachers and content-area teachers.

To successfully comprehend text, students should:

Prereading	• set a purpose for reading.
	• tap prior knowledge.
	• preview and predict what they will read.
During Reading	• look for key concepts and main ideas.
	• make inferences (hypotheses) and check them.
	• address comprehension problems as they arise.
Postreading	• confirm key concepts and main ideas.
	• reread if necessary.
	• review what they have read.

Prereading

Activities students engage in before reading help them prepare to learn new information. Preparing to read helps students incorporate what they read into their existing knowledge.

> **During prereading students should:**
> • identify key terms.
> • assess the level of difficulty and length of the selection.
> • gain a general sense of the topic and major subtopics.
> • understand text organization.
> • determine how this information relates to what they already know.

Here are some active learning behaviors that students should initiate before reading:

Consider why they are reading and create a plan for reading

This task requires students to think about why they are reading. What was the purpose of the assignment? If students are unclear, they need to find out why they are reading.

Next, students should look at the assignment to get a sense of how long and how difficult it is. Can they read the assignment in one session or should they break it into several sessions?

Think about what they know about the topic

Students who engage with the text create a scaffold for learning. When they bring prior knowledge to bear on their readings, students become involved with the text.

Preview the selection

When students preview, they think about what they already know about a topic and get a general idea of what they will learn. Students should:

- **Look at the title and subheadings.** These signal important ideas and usually hint at text organization.

- **Look at other graphic aids.** These include words within the text in italic or bold type, which may be vocabulary words or new concepts. Students should also look at aids such as maps and illustrations in the text.

- **Read the first and last paragraphs.** These often contain the thesis or major points of the reading. Remind students to connect what they are previewing with what they already know about the topic.

- **Read the first sentence or topic sentence of each paragraph.** Often, the main point of a paragraph is found at the beginning.

- **Get an idea of the text structure.** If students understand how the text is organized—for example, chronologically or in cause-and-effect form—they will be better able to follow the text.

During and Just-After Reading

The purpose of during and just-after reading behaviors is to turn passive readers into active readers. Active readers read metacognitively, monitoring their comprehension and "discussing" ideas with the author.

> **During reading students should:**
> - check their understanding of the selection.
> - use vocabulary techniques to understand new words.
> - relate each paragraph to the selection's main point.
>
> **Just after reading students should:**
> - relate what they read to what they already know.
> - adjust information gathered when previewing.

Read actively

To read actively, students should:

- **Think about why they are reading.** A person who is reading for pleasure reads differently from a person who is reading for information. Knowing *why* they are reading is critical to students' success. Students may learn their purpose in reading from their teacher, or they may understand the point of reading from experience in that subject.

Teaching Tip

Have students use previewing techniques with the selection you chose from your classroom text.

Teaching Tip

Model active reading using the selection you chose from your classroom text. Read one paragraph aloud and ask yourself some questions about the topic of the paragraph, the meaning of a term, or an author's opinion.

- **"Talk back" to the text.** Active readers stop often to ask themselves if they understand what they are reading. They agree or disagree with the author. They also identify the main points and supporting details of their reading.

- **Use text clues.** Remind students that readings often include clues about meaning, such as graphics, photographs, words in bold or italic type, headings, and the like. Headings, for example, signal a new subject or preview what will come next. Subheadings give information about the section.

- **Monitor their comprehension.** Successful readers monitor their understanding of the text. Most students need to be taught to pay attention not just to what they understand, but also to what they do *not* understand. When they are confused, they re-read the section looking for clues. If they're still unclear about meaning, they seek help.

Take notes

All of the strategies in the *Reading Strategies* series require students to take notes after they read. Notes help students retain what they learn. The process of writing important facts and details reinforces their importance and makes them easier to remember.

Teaching Tip

Demonstrate taking notes using the selection you chose from your classroom text.

There are many ways to take notes. Instruction in the *Reading Strategies* series focuses on several of them. Here are some guidelines for helping students take useful notes:

- **Taking good notes depends on selectivity.** Notes should contain only the most important points of the reading.

- **First, write the main points.** The main point may be in one paragraph or several. The process of deciding what a main point is spurs students to become active readers. Ask students what they think is the main point (or points) in a short selection from their textbook.

- **Next, write the supporting details.** The supporting details back up or tell more about the main point. Ask students what information they think supports the main point or points in the selection you chose.

Postreading

The final step for successful reading is reviewing. As with pre- and during-reading activities, postreading activities should become routine. There are many ways to review reading. Some are listed below. What they have in common is that the reader must synthesize the important points in the reading.

During postreading students should:
- synthesize the information they read.
- connect what they read to what they already knew.
- adjust their previewing techniques for use in future readings.
- form an opinion about what they have read.

Write a summary

This is the best-known strategy for postreading, and one with proven effectiveness. Introduce this skill in stages. When students first write a summary, suggest that they follow these guidelines:

- Keep the reading and the notes that students have taken to measure students' progress.

- Review notes on major points and supporting details before summarizing.

- Divide the writing into manageable sections, then summarize.

- Pay more attention to the content, less to the mechanics of writing.

- Try not to repeat the writer's words, but paraphrase them instead.

Engage in other postreading activities

Postreading activities can be adjusted to the purpose of the reading. Here are some additional suggestions:

- **Create a graphic organizer.** Making a graphic organizer can help students reorganize their notes to show text organization. See the section on graphic organizers in this book on pages T40–T47.

- **Give an oral summary.** To create a useful oral summary, the speaker has to state the key ideas and give examples so that the listener will understand. Consider asking student pairs to practice this technique by reading two different articles and summarizing them for each other.

- **Revisit predictions.** When they preview, students should make predictions about what they will read. After reading, students can think about what they expected when they previewed. How did what they actually learned differ from what they thought they might learn? Stress that predicting improves with practice and that there is no penalty for incorrect predictions. As students learn to analyze clues, their predictions will become more accurate.

- **Solve a problem; create a diagram.** Some readings may lend themselves to a type of review that is different from a summary. For example, a selection in a math textbook may be better reviewed by having students create new problems and then solve them. A process described in a science textbook may be more effectively reviewed by drawing a diagram. Suggest that students vary their review to suit the reading.

Reading in Social Studies

Many teachers discover that, while their students are adept at reading narrative texts, they do not understand social studies reading. They read a passage about a form of government looking for the next event in a plot, and miss the description of how the branches of that government interrelate. Mastering the particular demands of social studies can make a real difference in students' understanding of social studies topics.

The Demands of Reading in Social Studies

Students must understand several factors that characterize social studies textbooks. Primarily, these factors include text organization and the use of visuals, such as maps and other graphics. Students must also use critical-thinking skills for tasks such as distinguishing between primary and secondary sources and identifying an author's purpose.

Before students begin reading a selection, they should preview the textbook. A great deal of information often appears at the beginning and end of social studies textbooks, including an atlas, a glossary, lists of important facts, documents, and information about countries, movements, or philosophies. Remind students to refer to these aids as they read.

- **Recognizing fact and opinion** Students are faced with this issue in a variety of ways, including identifying propaganda. Help students identify phrases that signal opinions, such as *in my view* and *I believe,* and words that signal judgments, such as *better* and *more interesting.*

Teaching Tip

Primary sources often present special reading challenges because they may have a higher reading level than students' texts. Previewing is especially important, as is a slower reading rate. Students also might read documents in small groups.

- **Distinguishing between primary and secondary sources** Increasingly, students need to distinguish between primary and secondary sources. Explain that secondary sources reflect decisions made by the author about what is important and what events mean. Textbooks are usually secondary sources. Primary sources reflect the opinion of a single participant or may be the historical record, as in the case of a document such as the Declaration of Independence.

- **Critical thinking** Students need to be able to make inferences from facts, recognize cause-and-effect relationships, analyze an author's purpose, and draw conclusions.

- **Maps** Many social studies texts rely heavily on maps. Students can use maps actively by keeping one finger on the progress of a battle as they read. They can also draw their own maps. Make sure students understand how to read map legends.

- **Other visual aids** Most visual information in social studies texts clarifies or expands the topic. For example, a chart may summarize information in the text. Pictures may also provide primary source material. Captions often contain important information. Suggest that students read these aids more slowly than they would text because much information is included in a small space.

Text Structures in Social Studies

Understanding the text structure in social studies selections can make the task of reading social studies much easier. For example, when students understand that they are reading a chronological account, they can look for what is coming next and how that information fits into the whole. Common text structures in social studies include:

- **Main idea and details.** In this pattern, the intent is to explain a single topic. After identifying this pattern, students can look for the topic, the main points, and the supporting details. They can take notes in a wheel-and-spoke diagram.

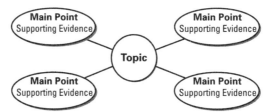

- **Comparison and contrast.** Social studies texts often compare two or more things, such as countries, leaders, or economic systems. Students can recognize this text structure through signal words such as *compared to* or *different from*. When students see this structure, they might record the differences and similarities they find in a Venn diagram.

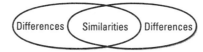

- **Sequence of events.** A timeline or a series of dates hints that a text is organized in a sequence of events. Demonstrate how to look for the next important event. Signal words include *first, next,* and *later.* Students may draw a timeline to record these events.

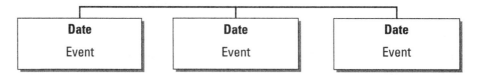

- **Cause and effect.** Identifying a cause-and-effect relationship prepares students both to predict what they may be reading next and to understand how it is related to a previous concept. A cause-and-effect graphic can help students grasp how key ideas and events are related.

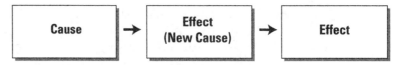

- **Combination of patterns.** Because a textbook will likely use several structures, students can benefit from careful previewing. A graphic representation of such a text structure may include several different drawings.

Teaching the Strategies

Students' success relies on their fully understanding how to apply the strategies with reading selections. In the Unit teaching notes, you will see teaching suggestions and think-alouds that you may wish to use to model for students the process of using strategies.

You may choose to teach these lessons to the entire class or to a group. You may also wish to divide the class into four groups and have each group focus on learning the strategy. When the groups feel confident, they might choose a selection to model the strategy for the rest of the class.

The graphic organizers in the Student Edition allow students to write a few responses in each step of the strategy. If you prefer to have students go into more depth, you might consider making copies of each strategy's reproducible graphic organizer for every student. These reproducibles are located on pages T41–T47 of this Annotated Teacher's Edition.

Unit 1 Strategy: **Outlining**
(pages 6–26)

Teaching Tip

Point out to students that because outlines highlight the main points of a topic, they can be used to review for tests.

Writing an outline is a good way to both plan a writing assignment and understand a reading selection. This is because a writer and a reader must identify the major points and the details or arguments that support each one. The outlining strategy works well with many kinds of readings because it does not require prior knowledge of the topic.

Introduce the Strategy
Tell students that many writers use outlines to help them plan the structure of their argument and gather the details they'll need. It makes sense, then, that readers could benefit from outlining, too. Point out that this strategy has three parts. First, students preview to get an idea of what the selection is about. Their next step is to read, then construct an outline of the main points and supporting details the writer has presented. Finally, they write a summary of the selection based on their outline.

The Strategy

I. Main Point
  A. Detail
  B. Detail
II. Main Point
  A. Detail
  B. Detail

Model the Strategy
If you are presenting this strategy to the whole class, draw the outline form on the board, make a copy for every student, or make an overhead transparency. You can use the reproducible on page T41 of this Annotated Teacher's Edition for this purpose. Model the strategy with students by making notes on the outline as you verbalize your thoughts.

As you model this strategy, point out the thoughts of the student who is using outlining to understand the selection. These appear on page 7 of the Student Edition in italic type. Tell students that they should use the outline form in the book and on the reproducible page as a guide. They may add more lines if needed, or they may use fewer lines than those in the form.

Have students follow along as you model the use of the outlining strategy with the lesson on pages 6–9 of the Student Edition.

Modeling Outlining

You may wish to use this or your own think-aloud plan to model using the outlining reading strategy.

Think-aloud Lesson Plan

Step 1. *The first thing I will do is preview the selection. The title tells me that this selection is about Sir Arthur Conan Doyle. He was the writer of the Sherlock Holmes mysteries. The photo on page 8 confirms this idea. The subtitles also seem to show that this is a biography and that it's written in time order.*

Next I'll read the first and last paragraphs and the topic sentences of every paragraph. In the first section, I see that Doyle was one of ten children, that he went to medical school, and that he was a ship's doctor. In the next section, I see that Doyle became an eye doctor, then he created Sherlock Holmes. Later, he became a war reporter. The last section tells me that after his wife died he became depressed. His reputation is alive today. Now I know that this is a biography of Doyle and that it's written in time order. I also know what parts of Doyle's life the writer will present.

Step 2. *Now I'll read to check my ideas and look for details about each part of Doyle's life. Let's read the biography together.*

[Read the biography with the class, either aloud or silently.]

Now I'll create my outline. I'll start with the outline the student began on page 9. It lists the details from the early part of Doyle's life. I see that he set up his outline with the subheadings on Roman-numeral lines and the details from each paragraph below. I'll continue his outline by listing the main ideas I found in each section. I'll put the main ideas on the capital-letter lines and the details that tell about each one on the numbered lines. My first entry will be on the "A" line in the "A Fork in the Road" section. I'll write that Doyle began writing the Sherlock Holmes stories after he became an eye doctor.

Step 3. *I'll use my outline to summarize what I've learned. I'll make sure to include all of the main points in my summary. I'll include one main point in each paragraph and add details that explain the point. The student began his summary on page 11 with Doyle's early life. I'll start the next paragraph by telling about how Doyle created Sherlock Holmes. When I'm finished, I'll keep the outline and summary to help me review the biography.*

Teaching Tip

You may wish to use only the Tree Map until students are able to successfully identify the main ideas and details of a selection. This graphic will be particularly accessible to ESL/LEP students.

Review the Strategy

Ask students what kind of writing they think they would find this strategy useful for. Suggest that it works well when there are clear main ideas, which are sometimes indicated by subheadings or bold type. Show students how using the outlining strategy gives them concrete proof that they have understood the selection, as well as material to review for a test.

An Alternative Method of Outlining

Because outlining requires higher-order thinking, you may wish to break down outline construction into a two-step process. You might ask students to identify the main ideas and details of a selection first, then create the hierarchy necessary to assembling an outline.

To do this, use the reproducible Tree Map on page T47 of this Annotated Teacher's Edition. Tree Maps allow students to concentrate on one task: identifying main ideas and details. Once these points have been identified, students can more easily construct a traditional outline.

Copy or make an overhead of the Tree Map for students. Encourage students to begin the map by writing one major point in each of the branching boxes. Then ask students to add details about each main point. Students might also wish to number the boxes on their map in pencil for easy reordering.

Their last step is to arrange the information in outline form. To simplify their task, you might suggest that students use the Roman-numeral, capital-letter, and, if needed, numbered lines only. They might add additional levels as their skills develop.

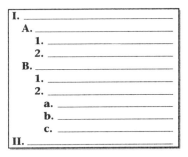

How To Use the Strategy

The following graphic demonstrates how outlining might work for a selection on early Japan.

> **Early Japan**
> I. Early peoples
>
>   A. First people: the Jomon
>
>   1. Lived between 8000 and 300 B.C.
>
>   2. Lived on Honshu Island
>
>   3. Hunted and fished for food
>
>   B. Next, the Yayoi
>
>   1. Replaced the Jomon about 200 B.C.
>
>   2. Planted rice and irrigated the land
>
> II. Heian Period: 794–1185 A.D.
>
>   A. Emperor Kammu made Heian (now Kyoto) capital of Japan
>
>   B. Kammu lost power to Fujiwara family in 858
>
>   1. Fujiwara family ruled for 300 years
>
>   2. Arts, writing, and poetry flourished

Summary: Japan's earliest people were the Jomons, who lived by hunting and fishing on Honshu Island between 8000 and 300 B.C. In 200 B.C., the Jomons were replaced by the Yayoi, who grew rice and introduced irrigation. In the Heian Period, Heian was renamed as Kyoto. In 858, Kammu lost power to the Fujiwara family, beginning 300 years when the arts flourished.

Lesson 1 (pages 10–13)
The Chocolate Journey

Selection Summary

This selection tells the story of the Columbian Exchange—how Christopher Columbus began the commerce between Europe and the Americas that led to the introduction of plants and animals to these regions and then around the world.

The introduction of chocolate to Europe began in 1502, when Columbus made his fifth voyage to the Americas and brought back cocoa. From the Americas also came pumpkins, tomatoes, sweet potatoes, squash, beans, and tobacco. From Europe, Columbus brought wheat, barley, sugar cane, horses, cows, and pigs. The "new" foods spread throughout the world.

Once Europeans began adding sugar to chocolate, the craze for the new food spread. Soon Europe became a world leader in chocolate production. Today, chocolate remains popular.

Strategy Notes

This selection can be divided up for an outline by using its subheadings; each is an indicator of a main point. Students may be confused by the fact that the article does not follow a strict chronological order, although that is its main structure.

There are digressions in the tale of chocolate, as when the author discusses the Columbian Exchange. Point out to students that although the section about the Columbian Exchange veers off from the main story about chocolate, it is an important point that deserves status as such in the outline.

Vocabulary Tip

The Vocabulary Tip on page 10 refers to the use of context clues to find the meaning of a new word. Refer students to Exercises 2 and 3 of Vocabulary Strategies for reinforcement of context clues.

ESL/LEP Notes

One way of helping keep track of the series of events in this selection is for ESL students to make themselves a timeline to go along with the outline. On this timeline, students should write the important dates mentioned in the article along with brief notes that explain the date's importance. These notes can be in either English or in the student's first language.

Extension

Students can do further research on the plants and animals that traveled to and from North America and Europe. Students can use this information to create a larger version of the map on the student page, drawing representations of the foods that traveled, including where they started and where they traveled to. Students can also plot some of Columbus's voyages on this map.

Lesson 2 (pages 14–17)
The "Ten Years Disaster"

Selection Summary

This selection consists of several firsthand accounts of the Cultural Revolution in China from about 1965–1975. During this period of terror, intellectuals, scientists, teachers, and the well-off—anyone suspected of anti-revolutionary thinking—were attacked physically and mentally. The Red Guard, mostly composed of young people, terrorized people and destroyed their houses and stores. Very little education went on during these years, and young and old people were sent to the country to be "re-educated," or indoctrinated into the accepted political opinions.

The accounts include one from a university student ostracized because of his father's "free-thinking." Another account is from a woman whose family had some money, so she was not allowed to join the Red Guard. Instead, she signed up to go to the country to prove her loyalty and almost died of starvation. A Red Guard explains that he deeply believed in what he was doing, until he thought about the attacks on good people in which he participated. A child, now grown, remembers seeing her father being shackled and jailed because of his views and feeling that her father could not protect her. A professor who believed deeply in the revolution explains how she, who had once taunted others, became a target.

Strategy Notes

Ask students how they might outline this article. Point out to students that in this case, the main points seem to be easily divided by subheadings. Explain that while this is not always a reliable way of determining structure, sometimes, as in this case, it does work.

ESL/LEP Notes

Suggest that students make sure they understand each section before they move on to the next one. Because the structure is so easy to discern, they can make sure they have the important details of each story. Check comprehension by asking students to tell you the important facts about one of these stories.

Extension

Students might want to fit the incidents discussed on a larger timeline that includes the important events occurring in China in the last 75 years. Students can work in pairs to research and complete these timelines. Then ask pairs to compare their work, creating a class timeline for modern China.

Lesson 3 (pages 18–20)
Ecotourism: Savior or Destroyer?

Selection Summary

The article begins with a description of ecotourism as its supporters see it: a cooperative venture in natural, wild places where both the tourists and the native people benefit. Supporters say ecotourism helps the economy by giving jobs to locals and preserving local arts. Ecotourism is sensitive to the environment and helps people of different cultures understand each other.

Those who disapprove of the concept say ecotourism can be more harmful than a huge resort, because the resort is isolated and does not affect the local residents the way ecotourism does. They also believe ecotourism can damage environments not otherwise visited at all and exploit the local people, who lose control of their heritage and their land.

Ecotourism has had some successes and some failures. The Kuna Indians in Panama failed because they did not have enough money to advertise. But in Ecuador, the Quicha developed a program based on their way of life that has proven enormously successful. Some groups have set guidelines for ecotourism, which include involving the local people to make sure their interests are considered.

Strategy Notes

Making an outline can be a difficult skill to acquire. However, it is very helpful once students are accustomed to using it. One discouraging aspect of making outlines for some students is that they sometimes misjudge what is an important point.

Help students identify main points by working with the class. Suggest that students use clues such as graphics, headings, and subheadings as they search for main points.

Write students' suggestions on the board. Have a discussion with the class, and get them to agree on what are the main points. Then discuss the supporting details. Finally, ask students to explain why they think these details support each main point.

Vocabulary Tip

The Vocabulary Tip on page 19 refers to the use of context clues to find the meaning of a new word. Refer students to Exercises 2 and 3 of Vocabulary Strategies for reinforcement of context clues.

ESL/LEP Notes

One way to judge students' understanding is to ask for an oral summary of the main points of the reading. Students should be able to tell you what ecotourism is, what its supporters and detractors say, what a successful and an unsuccessful program look like, and what the future of ecotourism is likely to hold. Students who can tell you that have a good understanding of this reading.

Lesson 4 (pages 21–24)
Should Women Vote?

Selection Summary

These essays present turn-of-the-century arguments for and against women's right to vote. The woman arguing against women's right to vote, Julia Shaw, believes that women's place is in the home. She thinks that women are not meant for the affairs of the world and would neglect their families if they got involved with voting. She argues that she does not have the information she needs to make good decisions and that women do not want to vote.

The debater in favor of women's right to vote, Charlotte Ramsey, says that women who want the vote are following in the footsteps of the country's founders, who believed in equality. She says that many educated and intelligent women are better equipped to vote than uneducated men are. She says that women earn money and pay taxes, and, because of this, they deserve to vote. Finally, she argues that the female point of view is essential in making good decisions in government.

Strategy Notes

It can be difficult for readers of historical documents to realize that the time in which a speech was written was a very different time with different understandings. Review the article with the students. Then have students talk about the structure of the article before they begin to outline. Ask students to explain how the article is organized. Have them try two different types of outlines: one based on using the subheadings and one based on finding other structural divisions (*e.g.*, they should consider dividing the article on the basis of the role of women in the home and the role of women in politics).

Vocabulary Tip

The Vocabulary Tip on page 22 refers to the use of context clues to find the meaning of a new word. Refer the students to Exercises 2 and 3 of Vocabulary Strategies for reinforcement of context clues.

ESL/LEP Notes

These speeches are written in a style that may be difficult for students to read. Because of this, you may want to pair English-language learners with students who are native speakers. Ask ESL students to ask their partners to explain phrases or words that are puzzling to them.

Extension

Debating can be a good way to engage students in historical subjects. Choose a topic that relates to the history students are learning and have them prepare both sides for a debate. You may even ask your class to brainstorm a list of topics to debate. The debate may either be similar to the one about women's right to vote, with two people simply stating their views in order. You may also choose a more traditional debate format, with each student giving an opening address, rebutting the other's argument, and then giving a closing argument.

Unit 2 Strategy: SQ3R
(pages 27–48)

(pages 27–48)

Teaching Tip

Before you begin this lesson, review page 1 of the Student Edition with students. This page discusses how to ask questions with informational text.

The Strategy

S = Survey
Q = Question
R = Read
R = Retell
R = Review

This is a long-used strategy that helps students set expectations for reading, ask questions based on their expectations, and read to find out if their expectations were accurate. Finally, students review their reading.

Introduce the Strategy

Explain that SQ3R stands for **S**urvey, **Q**uestion, **R**ead, **R**etell, and **R**eview. Show students the graphic on the overhead or the board, and ask students what each step might include. Tell students that when they survey, or preview, a reading, they read the title, subheadings, first and last paragraphs, and the topic sentences. They also look carefully at photos, illustrations, and captions, then they write their thoughts in the Survey box of their SQ3R chart.

After they survey, students should think about questions they have about the selection and write these questions in the Question box. This will help them set a purpose for reading. After reading, students should write in the Read box answers to their questions and any other important information they found. Next, they should review their reading by summarizing the selection in the Retell box. Finally, they should review what they have learned. This review may take several forms, depending on the selection. They might compare their SQ3R chart with a classmate's, check answers to their questions, or work a problem that uses a method presented in the selection.

Model the Strategy

If you are presenting this strategy to the whole class, draw the SQ3R graphic on the board, make a copy for every student, or make an overhead transparency. You can use the reproducible on page T42 of this Annotated Teacher's Edition for this purpose. Model the strategy with students by making notes on the SQ3R chart as you verbalize your thoughts.

When students use the SQ3R strategy, they create questions about what they would like to learn from the reading. Asking questions is a particularly difficult skill. Students often ask questions about minor details that do not help them discover the major ideas in the reading. Encourage students to develop their questioning skills by having them focus on *why* and *how* questions. These questions can help students understand the meaning of the entire selection.

Have students follow along as you model the use of the SQ3R strategy with the lesson on pages 27–30 of the Student Edition.

Think-aloud Lesson Plan

Step 1. *What do I know about the topic? I'll survey, or preview, the article. The title on page 28 and the photograph on page 29 tell me that the article is about the re-release of the movie* Star Wars. *I see that the student who began the SQ3R chart on page 27 wrote that she wondered if the reviewer would say that the movie still looked good. I've seen* Star Wars, *so I know what it's about. It has aliens, spaceships, and chase scenes.*

I'll read the first and last paragraphs and the topic sentence of each paragraph to see what the reviewer says. I see that the reviewer still thinks that Star Wars *is a good movie. Now I'll make notes on what I know about the movie in the Survey column.*

Teaching Tip

If students' questions are not answered in the selection, suggest that they first reread the article to check. If they still don't find answers, suggest that they go to the library or to the Internet to look for additional information.

Step 2. *My next step is to make up some questions about the re-release of* Star Wars. *I want to know if it's worth spending money on a movie ticket. I've already rented it. I'll add that to the Question column of the chart on the top of page 28.*

Step 3. *As I read, I'll think about what I've written in the Survey and Question boxes and look for answers to the questions I wrote. Let's read the article together.*

[Read the article with the class, either aloud or silently.]

Now I'll take notes about what I learned. I'll also try to answer the questions I wrote. I see that in the chart on the bottom of page 30, the student wrote the special effects are still good. I'll write that even though I've seen the movie on a TV screen, the reviewer says that the big screen is more exciting because the airships are life-sized and the reactions of the other moviegoers add to the fun.

Step 4. *Now I'll retell what I've learned so I'll remember it. I learned that* Star Wars *is still a terrific movie and that movies are different today. I'll add some details about why it's still a great movie: The special effects are terrific, the story is still fun, and it's worth paying to see it on the big screen.*

Step 5. *Finally, I'll review what I've learned by talking with my brother about the movie. Maybe I can convince him to go see it with me.*

Review the Strategy

Ask students to practice this strategy on another reading assignment. As they work, tell students to ask questions to clarify what they do not understand. This will help them feel comfortable with using the strategy on their own.

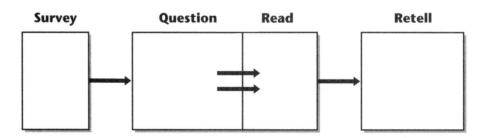

Survey   **Question**   **Read**   **Retell**

How To Use the Strategy

The following graphic demonstrates how the SQ3R strategy might work for a selection on the founding of the Massachusetts colony in North America.

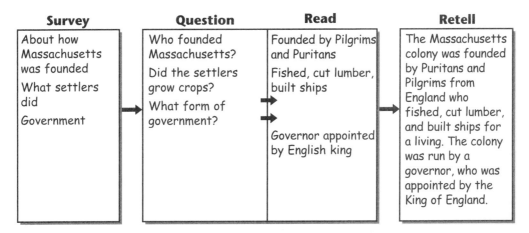

Survey	Question	Read	Retell
About how Massachusetts was founded What settlers did Government	Who founded Massachusetts? Did the settlers grow crops? What form of government?	Founded by Pilgrims and Puritans Fished, cut lumber, built ships Governor appointed by English king	The Massachusetts colony was founded by Puritans and Pilgrims from England who fished, cut lumber, and built ships for a living. The colony was run by a governor, who was appointed by the King of England.

Lesson 5 (pages 31–34)
When the Rains Wouldn't Come

Selection Summary

This diary focuses on the experiences of a young person living through the Dust Bowl in Oklahoma in 1934. The writer experiences the fear of living in an agricultural area during this time when the sky brought only blazing sun, and the wind only dust. The diary writer lives through the family decision to leave for California and the process of packing up belongings and driving off for what the family hopes will be a new, more prosperous life. The diary ends, however, with the realization that there may be few jobs in California.

Strategy Notes

The SQ3R strategy is based on the ability of students to look for clues to help them become familiar with the article. In this case, students may have only a vague idea of what the Dust Bowl is. Students can use the illustration to help them learn about the Dust Bowl.

As students survey the article, they can easily see that the writing is organized into diary entries that cover several months. When they survey, students set a purpose for reading. In this case, students' purpose should be to understand more about what it was like to live through the Dust Bowl. Remind students that as they survey, they should think about questions they might have about the selection.

ESL/LEP Notes

Students who have not grown up in this country may have few ideas about this period of U.S. history. You can facilitate their understanding by pointing them to the photo of the Dust Bowl on page 32 of the Student Edition.

Point out that the Dust Bowl diary was written in the middle of the Great Depression, a time in which economic hardship was common in this country. Then ask students to brainstorm about what the Dust Bowl might have been and how it might have affected the lives of the people.

Extension

Ask students to choose another member of the diary writer's family and write an entry based on what that person might be experiencing. Students may want to read their entries to the class or in small groups and compare the entries they wrote.

Lesson 6 (pages 35–38)
The Celebration Experiment

Selection Summary

The Disney corporation has embarked on an experiment: The company is building a town called Celebration in Florida. This new town is heartily endorsed by those who see Disney as a wholesome, well-managed enterprise; those who consider the corporation a manipulative, boring enemy think the new town will be a disaster.

Walt Disney first came up with the idea of a Disney town many years ago; this version is less futuristic and more reminiscent of older neighborhoods. There is no city government in Celebration. Instead, Disney runs the government. There is no shortage of buyers for the houses in the new community because many like the idea of no government. City planners are waiting to see how the future of this new kind of city unwinds.

Strategy Notes

Some students may need help in determining what information they have about a topic for an SQ3R chart. Suggest to students that they may not know much about the Disney town. However, they probably know something about Disney. Ask them to think about what they know about Disney. You might try asking them to brainstorm while you write their thoughts on the board.

Then have them survey the article. After they complete their survey, have students form questions from their ideas. For example, they might ask: What kind of town might a company like Disney build? These connections between prior knowledge and predictions can give students a head start when they read.

ESL/LEP Notes

One technique that can be useful for English-language learners is to approach instruction from a variety of angles. For example, in trying to make sure that students understand the steps of the strategy, you can try asking them to restate these steps to you. If the student does not understand, try rephrasing the steps or repeating them and asking students to stop when they do not understand.

Internet Connection

http://disney.go.com
This site discusses everything that is Disney, including movies, books, music, merchandise, and magazines. It includes details about current events, plans, and changes taking place at the Walt Disney Company.

Lesson 7 (pages 39–42)
The Race for Longitude

Selection Summary

For centuries, sea voyages were dangerous because no one had established a reliable way to determine longitude, the distance east or west of a given point. The ideas of longitude and latitude are old; Ptolemy, the Greek scientist, plotted these imaginary lines on maps.

Sailors could plot latitude, the distance north or south of the equator, by measuring the sun and the stars and their relation to the ship. Determining longitude was trickier. Sailors needed to know the exact time at home and compare this to when it was noon on the ship. This was difficult in the 18th century, because clocks were unreliable.

So important was solving the problem, though, that England offered a prize of about $12 million. Many vied for the prize using two methods. One was finding a way to use astronomy to find longitude. The other was building a better clock. After many trials and after being dismissed because he championed the less-elegant clock solution, clockmaker John Harrison solved the problem and won the prize.

Strategy Notes

In this selection, surveying is crucial to getting a head start on understanding, since students are not likely to know much about the longitude prize. Encourage students to carefully survey and note what this selection is about. You might want to model this strategy by saying, *As I survey, I see that the selection deals with latitude and longitude, those imaginary lines that help us locate places on a map. There's something here about the history of finding these measurements at sea and that they're important for sailors. I see England offered a prize to find longitude and that people tried different ways.*

Discuss how surveying can help students get ready to understand a topic. You also might want to have students divide into two groups to practice surveying. Have the groups present their findings to the class and discuss any differences.

Vocabulary Tip

The Vocabulary Tip on page 41 refers to the use of context clues to find the meaning of a new word. Refer students to Exercises 2 and 3 of Vocabulary Strategies for reinforcement of context clues.

ESL/LEP Notes

English-language learners can benefit from being told instructions in several ways. Try going through the selection with these students, explaining each step of the strategy in different ways—rephrasing it, drawing pictures, and so on—to enhance understanding. You might want to have students repeat the instructions back to you so you can check their comprehension.

Extension

Ask students to use different strategies with this selection and then write a summary. Ask volunteers to read their summary to the class. Then discuss whether the different strategies resulted in different understandings and if one strategy seemed to work better than the others.

Internet Connection

http://www.southpole.com/qanda.html
Janice and Randy are making seven stops on their way to the South Pole. Can your students identify their stops based only on their latitude and longitude? This is just one of the activities The South Pole Adventure Web Page has to offer. It provides definitions and explanations of latitude and longitude and offers students activities that reinforce this information.

Lesson 8 (pages 43–46)
A Debate on Slavery

Selection Summary

These newspaper editorials from about 1850 show the pro and con sides of the slavery debate. The writer taking the pro position lists the reasons he believes in slavery: Enslaved people are more like children than adults and would be lost without supervision. Because they come from a world where slavery is common and where they were probably enslaved, the system is one they understand. They are happy, well-treated, -housed, and -fed. If they were to be set free, they would suffer and feel it a punishment. No one is free, but enslaved people at least are happy in their place. The South would suffer greatly if slavery were to end.

The opponent to slavery states that the Founding Fathers were right and that all men are created equal, not as some enslaved and some free. Enslaved people were torn from their families, and their bodies and souls were sold. Their lives are horrible, with not enough food, poor housing, and treatment that includes being shackled and beaten. Who are slaveholders to decide the fate of another human? Slavery is morally wrong, and the United States must end it so that its citizens can hold their heads high.

Strategy Notes

Suggest that students consider how best to represent the information in these two essays within the SQ3R graphic. Discuss the benefits of making one graphic for each side of the issue or of dividing one graphic in half.

You can also suggest that students try a different graphic. For example, they might try a Venn diagram or a structure in which each writer's points are answered by the other writer. Stress to students that the graphics are intended to aid understanding. If students find another graphic that works better, they should use it.

Vocabulary Tip

The Vocabulary Tip on page 44 refers to the use of context clues to find the meaning of a new word. Refer students to Exercises 2 and 3 of Vocabulary Strategies for reinforcement of context clues.

ESL/LEP Notes

Model what a completed SQ3R graphic might look like by working with English-language learners on using the strategy to understand this article. Ask students to explain the steps as they are going through them, jumping in to offer modeling suggestions when necessary.

Extension

Ask students to use the format of this reading to create a debate of their own. Have the class decide on a topic that interests them and prepare to argue either side of the debate. Then call students' names at random and ask them to engage in five-minute debates about the topic. Give each student a one-minute opener and another one-minute rebuttal, with a 30-second closing argument.

Unit 3 Strategy: **PLAN**

(pages 49–68)

(pages 49–68)

Teaching Tip

This strategy may be particularly useful for visual learners, in that they can design their own graphic organizer. Students' designs will also demonstrate how they have interpreted the text.

The Strategy

P = Predict
L = Locate
A = Add
N = Note

PLAN stands for Predict, Locate, Add, and Note. This strategy relies on students to choose a graphic organizer to map the selection or to create a graphic of their own. Students who think best in pictures find this strategy useful because it allows them to schematically represent the ideas they encounter in the text.

Introduce the Strategy

Tell students that before writers write, they map out their ideas. They think about how they will present their arguments. They think about how they will organize their writing. They decide if they will focus on explaining one topic, if they will compare topics, or if they will organize their work in some other way, such as presenting events in the order in which they occurred or as a series of causes and effects.

Then explain what the acronym PLAN represents. Tell students that, as in the other reading strategies taught in this book, they will preview the reading to predict what they will read. They will also decide how the text is organized so that they can choose a word map, or graphic organizer, to map what they learn.

Their next step is to write their predictions on their word map. They will then locate these ideas on the map, making check marks next to ideas they know about and question marks next to ideas they're unfamiliar with. After they read, they will add information about their predictions. Finally, they will note what they have learned by reviewing.

Model the Strategy

If you are presenting this strategy to the whole class, draw the three PLAN graphics on the board or make overhead transparencies of all three organizers. You can use the reproducibles on pages T43–T45 of this Annotated Teacher's Edition for this purpose. Model the strategy by choosing a graphic organizer with students. Then, if you choose, distribute copies of the chosen organizer to every student. Make notes on the organizer as you verbalize your thoughts.

Show how each graphic might be useful for a different kind of writing—a Venn diagram for a reading that compares two things, a wheel-and-spoke diagram for a reading with one main topic, and a sequence chart for a reading that is organized in chronological order or as a series of causes and effects.

Have students follow along as you model the use of the PLAN strategy with the lesson on pages 49–52 of the Student Edition.

Modeling PLAN

You may wish to use this or your own think-aloud plan to model using the PLAN reading strategy.

Think-aloud Lesson Plan

Step 1. *The first thing I'll do is to look at the title, photo, caption, first and last paragraphs, and topic sentences. The title and photo show me that I'll learn about Koko, who is a talking gorilla, and someone named Dr. Patterson. The topic sentences show me that this whole article will be about Koko, so I'll use the wheel-and-spoke diagram to map what I learn. I'll write Koko's name in the central circle because that's the topic of the selection. Then I'll write what I've learned from previewing in the outside circles.*

Teaching Tip

Tell students that if their graphic organizer doesn't fit the selection, they should simply discard it and try another organizer.

On page 50, I see the student made the same choice. She wrote "mountain gorilla" and "Dr. Patterson" in the outside circles. I'll add some circles and some details. The first paragraph tells me that animals can communicate, so I predict that the article will tell me about how Koko communicates with people.

Step 2. *I know something about this topic because I've noticed how my dog tells me when she's hungry, so I'll write a check mark in that circle. Like the student, I don't know about Dr. Patterson, so I'll leave the question mark there.*

Step 3. *Now I'll read the article to learn more about Koko and Dr. Patterson. As I read, I'll look for more information about how Koko talks. Let's read the article together.*

[Read the article with the class, either aloud or silently.]

Now I'll add information to my word map about what I learned in my reading. I learned that Koko can communicate by using American Sign Language. She doesn't just sign to show that she wants something either. She understood when Dr. Patterson told her that her kitten had been killed, and she cried.

Teaching Tip

Point out that students' completed word map will show the article's main ideas and details. You can use the graphic to assess students' understanding of their reading.

Step 4. *I've now completed my word map, so I'll review what I've learned. I've learned that gorillas and humans belong to the same genetic family and that Dr. Patterson taught sign language to Koko as an experiment. I've also learned that Koko was the first gorilla to learn a human language and that Dr. Patterson started the Gorilla Foundation to help save wild mountain gorillas. I'll keep my PLAN word map so I can review this article later.*

Review the Strategy

Remind students that when they use this strategy, they have a choice in what kind of graphic they use. Also tell them that not every idea for a graphic organizer will work. For example, students find when they read that the text is organized in time order, not as a main idea with details. In that case, they should start again with a different graphic. Also, they should feel free to modify the graphics presented. Additional circles or lines will be necessary to accommodate different selections.

You might also want to check students' understanding of the PLAN strategy by having them practice it with different types of text organizations. Encourage students to create graphic organizers of their own and to present and explain them to the class.

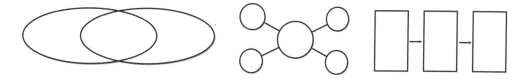

How To Use the Strategy

The following graphic demonstrates how the PLAN strategy might work for a selection on overland routes to the West.

Summary: Five trails led through the West. One was the Cumberland Road, which went from Maryland to Illinois. Construction began on this route in 1811. Another route was the Oregon Trail, which led from Missouri to Oregon, and was first used in 1812. The trip took 5 months. The Santa Fe Trail connected Independence, Missouri, and Santa Fe. It passed through a desert. The Old Spanish Trail was created by a Mexican trader. It went from Santa Fe to Los Angeles. Finally, the California Trail went from Idaho to San Francisco, branching off the Oregon Trail.

Lesson 9 (pages 53–55)
The Underground Railroad

Selection Summary

This historical piece delves into the history and effects of the Underground Railroad, the path by which enslaved people in the South escaped to freedom in the northern states or Canada. Escapees, who traveled by night, traveled between farms, called "stations," that agreed to hide them. Some of the "conductors" were white; others were free African Americans.

Harriet Tubman was one famous conductor on the Underground Railroad. Tubman escaped to the North and then led 300 escapees to freedom. The Underground Railroad helped stir sympathy for enslaved people and the lives they led. Indirectly, it led to the Civil War, through both the outrage in the North and the anger in the South of slaveholders who felt that their "property" was being stolen from them.

Strategy Notes

To help students use the PLAN strategy with this selection, remind them that they can choose any graphic they wish. If students seem unsure how to choose a graphic, review some possibilities with them.

Is the piece organized so one event follows another, which would indicate a sequence chart? Is the piece contrasting two or more things, in which case a Venn Diagram would work well? Is the writing constructed so there are several minor ideas that all have to do with a main idea? In that case, a wheel-and-spoke diagram would work well. If students do not think any of these would work, suggest they create their own graphic.

ESL/LEP Notes

English language learners may also be acquiring the background in U.S. history that most native speakers have. You may wish to give ESL students some background in the causes and effects of the Civil War to help them put this piece in context.

Curriculum Connections: Language Arts

The story of the escapees on the Underground Railroad is a dramatic one; suggest that interested readers check out from a library a book called *Follow the Drinking Gourd,* an easy-to-read, short novel by Jeanette Winter that follows runaway escapees as they travel north to freedom on the Underground Railroad.

Internet Connection

http://www.history.rochester.edu/class/ugrr/home.htm
This site offers a detailed explanation of the history behind and the effects of the Underground Railroad. It discusses the functions of the Underground Railroad, and how the enslaved persons were transported and helped to gain their freedom.

Lesson 10 (pages 56–58)
America's Secret Weapon in World War II

Selection Summary

The idea for the Navajo Code Talkers came from a man named Philip Johnson, who had grown up on a Navajo reservation. Johnson knew the Marines were looking for a code that the Japanese could not break. He also knew that the Navajo language was extremely difficult and known by only about thirty people who were not Navajo.

Johnson proposed that the Navajo language be used as the basis for a code. In an experiment, the idea worked. Two Navajo speakers relayed messages, and no one was able to understand what they were saying. Four hundred Navajos served as Code Talkers in World War II, and the Japanese never did decipher what they were saying. In the battle of Iwo Jima, six Code Talkers worked around the clock. Without them, according to one officer, "the Marines would never have taken Iwo Jima."

Strategy Notes

In this selection, you might want to ask students to experiment with making their own graphic organizer for the PLAN strategy. First, ask them to preview the selection and think about how it is organized. Then ask them to visualize how that structure might be made into a word picture.

Ask students to draw some ideas, and then have a class discussion in which students show their organizer and discuss why it might or might not work. You might want to collect the students' suggested organizers, or make a copy of them, to keep in a folder for future reference. You might also ask students to present and explain their designs to the class.

Vocabulary Tip

The Vocabulary Tip on page 57 refers to the use of context clues to find the meaning of a new word. Refer students to Exercises 2 and 3 of Vocabulary Strategies for reinforcement of context clues.

ESL/LEP Notes

To gauge the level of understanding English-language learners have of this selection, ask them in a one-on-one setting to summarize the article. While you listen, watch for understanding of the main points of the article, that the student is able to grasp how the Code Talkers got started, why the system worked well, and the role of the Code Talkers in World War II. If students are unable to give you a clear summary, work with a small group to follow the steps of the strategy together.

Extension

Give students more practice with using the PLAN strategy by asking them to use the strategy on a reading assignment from your class or another class.

Before students begin, ask them to state the steps of the PLAN strategy. As students tell them to you, write them on the board. Then ask students to use the strategy when they read.

Encourage students to raise their hands and ask questions about the strategy as they work. After students finish, discuss what works in the strategy and what doesn't. Does the strategy help them remember more and understand better what they have read? If not, how could they use the strategy so it worked better?

Internet Connection

http://www.history.navy.mil/faqs/faq12-1.htm This Naval Historical Center site answers frequently asked questions people have about the Code Talkers in World War II. It includes why the code talkers were developed, what they were required to do, and how they translated words.

Lesson 11 (pages 59–62)
The "Glory That Was Greece"

Selection Summary

This selection focuses on the government of ancient Greece—its origins, its history, and its importance to our form of government. Ancient Greece began about 1900 B.C., when nomadic herders began to settle in city–states. The government of a city–state generally went through these stages: the age of kings, oligarchy (rule of the few), tyranny, and finally, beginning democracy. Ancient Greece usually refers to Athens, which was rich because of the control of its navy. Although Athens was rich, many in the city–state were slaves. Those who were free had time to paint, sculpt, and think about philosophy.

Strategy Notes

Point out the series of bulleted items in the piece. Ask students why they should pay attention to them. Students should say that the bullets highlight important ideas or events. Tell students that in their textbooks, they will often see examples of lists and bulleted items called out from text with boldface or italic type. These graphic devices prompt readers to pay attention and signal that the information they are reading is important.

ESL/LEP Notes

This selection has many terms that may be unfamiliar to students. Encourage students to make a separate list of words they do not understand and write them in a notebook divided by subject. That allows students to keep an ongoing list of new terms. Continue to draw

students' attention to these terms as the year progresses. Learning words this way—words students themselves have written—can help them build their English vocabulary.

Extension

Students can choose another ancient society to research and write about. Students should focus on different governmental structures that existed in these ancient civilizations and how these governments either differ or relate to modern governments. Encourage students to make a graphic of the organization of the ancient governments they study and display it for the class.

Lesson 12 (pages 63–66)
Living at the Mall

Selection Summary

This selection addresses both the history and the potential future of the shopping mall. It begins by describing the town square of years past, which was replaced by shopping malls in the 1920s and 1930s. Over the years, shopping malls have become increasingly insulated from the outside world and from the communities in which they are housed. Today, some developers are trying to bring back the idea of a town square, albeit in a shopping mall. These planners want to include post offices, libraries, and other community activities to create a new center for the communities that right now only have shopping malls. Some planners and community activists, however, say it is too late to save many downtowns.

Strategy Notes

There are few students in the United States who have not visited shopping malls. This article, then, is a good one to use to emphasize the idea of predicting what you will read based on what you know.

Work with students to help them choose a graphic. Ask students to preview the article and think about what they already know about malls. Students can draw their graphics with their predictions. After students complete their graphics, ask them to look again at their predictions. How close were they? How did writing these predictions help them become more involved in what they were reading? Tell students that there is no penalty for incorrect predictions. Stress that predicting skills improve as students increase their ability to preview accurately.

ESL/LEP Notes

If you discover that English-language learners are having trouble understanding not only the material but also the instructions you offer, try approaching instruction from a variety of angles. For example, ask students to restate the steps of the strategy to you so you can make sure they understand them. If students still do not understand, try rephrasing the steps and asking students to stop you and ask for clarification when they do not understand.

Cooperative Learning

Ask students to think about the article they just read with the idea of creating a shopping mall that could serve as a town square for students. Ask students to work in teams to design and draw a floor plan layout for a shopping center/town square for teenagers.

Unit 4 Strategy: PACA

(pages 69–89)

(pages 69–89)

When they make predictions, students should think about the *hows* and *whys* of the selection to help them find the main points of the text.

PACA stands for **P**redicting **A**nd **C**onfirming **A**ctivity. This strategy works well on readings that have topics about which students have some background knowledge. With this information, students can make appropriate predictions. When readers make predictions, they develop an investment in the reading— they want to read to find out if their predictions were accurate.

Introduce the Strategy

Explain what the acronym PACA represents. Then ask students what kind of reading they think this strategy would be best for. Students may say that it would work best for a topic about which they have some prior knowledge.

Suggest to students that they may have some prior knowledge about a topic even if they do not know a great deal about it. They also can develop prior knowledge about a topic by previewing the reading. In this way, they will get a general sense of the topic so that they will be able to make some predictions about what they will read.

The Strategy

P = Predicting
A = And
C = Confirming
A = Activity

Model the Strategy

If you are presenting this strategy to the whole class, draw the PACA graphic on the board, make a copy for every student, or make an overhead transparency. You can use the reproducible on page T46 of this Teacher's Resource Manual for this purpose. Model the strategy with students by making notes on the PACA chart as you verbalize your thoughts.

Explain what students will write in each section of the PACA graphic: They will write predictions in the Predictions column. They will write check marks in the small box in the corner of a prediction that proved to be correct. They will revise predictions that were incorrect and write stars in the small box of those predictions. If they cannot revise a prediction, they will cross it out. In the Support column, they will write details that explain each prediction.

Emphasize that there are no penalties for incorrect predictions. Students must develop their ability to use clues to make correct predictions. Even experienced readers make incorrect predictions at times, especially if the topic is unfamiliar or if the author's ideas are unexpected or new. Students' aim is to make increasingly accurate predictions by honing their ability to detect clues when previewing.

Have students follow along as you model the use of the PACA strategy with the lesson on pages 69–72 of the Student Edition.

Modeling PACA

You may wish to use this or your own think-aloud plan to model using the PACA reading strategy.

Think-aloud Lesson Plan

Step 1. *First, I'll think about what I know about in-line skating. I see kids doing it. They really seem to like it. I know that it looks like a cross between ice skating and roller skating. I know that some skaters seem to go very fast.*

I'll preview the reading to see what it will tell me. I'll look at the title, the subheadings, the first and last paragraphs, the topic sentences, and any photos. The first paragraph of the section explains how in-line skating might have started. The picture shows an in-line skater wearing protective gear. He seems to be flying through the air.

I see the student who has begun the PACA chart on page 69 predicted that the article will talk about the history of in-line skating. The student also predicts that the article will talk about how to skate in races.

Teaching Tip

Students should think about the reasons an author gives for any opinions he or she presents. Evaluating opinions will help students learn to support their own predictions with facts.

Step 2. *Now I'll read the article. As I read, I'll look for my predictions to see if I was right. I'll also look to see why my predictions were right—or wrong. Let's read the article together.*

[Read the article with the class, either aloud or silently.]

Step 3. *I'll look back at the PACA chart to check my predictions. I see that the student has checked one of her predictions in the chart on page 70. She crossed out the prediction that said "how to skate in races" because she realized that the writer didn't talk about that. Instead, she wrote "how to skate safely" and put a star in the small box. The small star will remind her that this is a corrected prediction. Then she's added support for her predictions in the Support column.*

Review the Strategy

Ask students to practice this strategy on another reading assignment (or you might want to choose an appropriate selection). As they work, tell students to feel free to ask questions to clarify what they do not understand. This will help them feel comfortable with using the strategy again on their own.

Predictions	Support

How to Use the Strategy

The following graphic demonstrates how the PACA strategy might work for a selection on reproduction without seeds.

Predictions		Support
Stems can reproduce without seeds.	✓	Tubers, bulbs, corms are underground stems that reproduce.
~~All reproduction without seeds based on stems or roots~~		
Leaves can reproduce.	★	Some plants produce little plantlets to reproduce.

Lesson 13 (pages 73–76)
Caught in the Blitz

Selection Summary

This letter traces the writer's experiences in the Blitz in London during World War II, when Germany bombed London night after night. The letter mentions how the letter-writer protected himself, what it was like to live through the Blitz, and how people eventually learned to live with the constant bombing. Finally, the author writes, people stopped taking as many precautions.

Strategy Notes

You could use this selection as the center of a comprehension workshop. Explain that students should feel free to ask questions about how to employ the strategy. Ask student volunteers to read the opening paragraphs of the letter. Then tell them to use the strategy while reading the selection.

As students read and then take notes, watch how they fill in the graphic. Offer suggestions to students who are having trouble understanding how to make predictions and confirm them. If students are still having problems, pair them with students who have mastered the techniques of using this strategy.

Vocabulary Tip

The Vocabulary Tip on page 73 refers to the use of context clues to find the meaning of a new word. Refer students to Exercises 2 and 3 of Vocabulary Strategies for reinforcement of context clues.

ESL/LEP Notes

Even though students may not be familiar with this topic, the letter is written in a way that emphasizes the feelings and reactions of the person living through the Blitz. Regardless of their background, students should be able to understand the writer's emotions and understand what happened to him. Gauge English-language learners' understanding of this writing by asking them to write a summary of what happened to Jeremy as outlined in his letter. Outlines should contain information about the start of the Blitz, how it continued, and Jeremy's reaction to the constant bombardment.

Extension

This selection is in the form of a letter. Ask students to choose another literary form—a diary, a play, a radio broadcast, a short story, or any other form—and to restate the information from the letter in that new form. Students may need to do additional research for this project. When students have finished their work, ask them to share it. Discuss how information can be manipulated, and discuss the impressions that come across in these different forms of text.

Internet Connection

http://www.cfcsc.dnd.ca/links/milhist/wwii.html
This site offers a comprehensive index of topics about World War II, including information about aerial operations, art and literature, the atomic bomb, campaigns and battles, the Holocaust, media and propaganda, organizations and programs, personal narratives, war crimes, and women and the war.

Lesson 14 (pages 77–80)
The Silk Road

Selection Summary

The Silk Road, which runs between China and Europe, was for 1,600 years the overland route between these two continents. The 5,000-mile trade route offered travelers dangers that ranged from avalanches to terrifying passes and from oppressive cold and heat to bandits. For many, though, the risks were worth the trip.

Travelers on the Silk Road carried silk to Europe, which paid its weight in gold. The Silk Road, which became active in 100 B.C., began in Changan. From there, travelers had to cross the Takla Makan, a deadly desert that ended at the treacherous cliffs of the Pamir Mountains. Then they went on to Europe.

Marco Polo was one famous traveler on the Silk Road who spent years in China and wrote about his adventures in a famous book. Perhaps the most important result of the Silk Road was the connection it made between the cultures of Europe and Asia—a connection that was the beginning of understanding between the continents.

Strategy Notes

A map that accompanies a geography selection is almost always critical to understanding. Often such a map either reinforces the main point of the selection or it can serve as a handy guide to the reading. In this case, the route the map traces is the subject of the article. By looking at this map, students can make better predictions. Reinforce this point to students by showing them other instances in their textbooks and in other books where graphics, particularly maps, are both critical to understanding and contain a capsule of the article.

ESL/LEP Notes

Suggest that as students read this selection, they keep one finger on the map as they read. By moving their finger to the geographic locations as they are mentioned within the text, students will have another way of reinforcing the message of the words.

Extension

Students can compare the map in the lesson with a contemporary map of Asia and Europe and choose countries to research. Arrange for students to choose one country the Silk Road passed through and ask them to describe the geography, culture, and government of their country. Have students present the countries in order, so the class can get a good sense of what the travelers experienced on their journey on the Silk Road.

Lesson 15 (pages 81–83)
Tragedy at Kent State

Selection Summary

This selection discusses the killing of four Kent State college students in 1970. The article begins with a brief overview of the Vietnam War—the Communists fighting a civil war with pro-government troops in Vietnam that the U.S. government feared the Communists would win. This led to U.S. troops in Vietnam and the escalation of U.S. involvement.

By 1968, student protests were common. Antiwar protests at Kent State in Ohio began in April 1970, after President Nixon announced the war was expanding. Violence broke out May 1; windows were smashed downtown. The Ohio governor brought in the National Guard to keep order. The next night, 100 students gathered to protest, and the ROTC building was set on fire. The next day, when students would not end a rally, the National Guard fired tear gas into the crowd.

Two thousand people gathered on May 4, and the confrontation with the National Guard escalated. Then the Guard fired into the crowd, killing four students. Kent State, and finally 200 other universities, were shut down.

Commissions disagreed about who was at fault in the shootings. Twenty years after the deaths, Kent State built a memorial; on a plaque nearby are the names of the dead and injured students. Veterans groups also planted a daffodil for each soldier killed in the war.

Strategy Notes

Students may have vague ideas about Kent State and what happened there. Ask them to use those vague ideas, as they look at the photograph, the title and subheadings, the first and last paragraphs, and the topic sentences to get a sense of what they predict would be in this selection.

Stress that an active reader makes predictions about what he or she will read based on many things. For example, readers can predict the episode is an unhappy one from the title; the subheadings tell readers that the events in this selection will follow more or less chronologically. Students may also know something about what happened and add that information to the clues they already have. It is this often unconscious melding of information from several sources that helps active readers get an idea of what they might expect as they read.

ESL/LEP Notes

The Vietnam War did not have the universal interest outside this country that conflicts such as World Wars I and II did; because of that, some English-language learners may have few resources to draw on to understand this conflict and this selection. Suggest to these students that they find out more to get a better context for the importance of the Vietnam War in America. There are several ways to do this. Students can find more information in encyclopedias or ask other students who are knowledgeable about U.S. history to explain more about why this war meant so much to Americans.

Extension

Timelines can be an aid in reading history. In this case, students can benefit from two different timelines. One can focus on the events surrounding the Vietnam War. Ask students to use the dates given in the selection and add other important dates they research. The other timeline should be of the dates involved in the dispute at Kent State between the government and the student protesters. Under each day of the protests, students should list the events in the order in which they happened.

Lesson 16 (pages 84–87)
Journey Down the Unknown River

Selection Summary

John Wesley Powell explored the Colorado River in 1869, when no one was sure what lay in wait on the river as it flowed through the Grand Canyon. This soldier convinced his old friend, President Ulysses S. Grant, to help fund an expedition. Powell and his men thought the trip might last ten months. They packed for that. The extra food and supplies came in handy, though, when the boats crashed and they lost food.

The men ran enormous rapids, scaled the cliffs by the river, and more than once were sure they would die as they plunged blindly over waterfalls in their battered boats. The river runners made it through safely, however, becoming the first to traverse this treacherous stretch of the Colorado River by boat.

Strategy Notes

Part of becoming an active reader is learning both to preview before reading and to notice the clues that signal what to expect while reading. Tell students to look at the subheadings. Ask them what kind of information they might expect to find in each of these sections. Point out that students who make predictions based on these kinds of clues will have a head start when they begin reading. They will be able to anticipate what is coming and be ready to respond to it.

ESL/LEP Notes

Suggest that English-language learners create their own dictionaries with English words they encounter but do not understand, such as: *apprehensive, tales, expedition,* and *rapids.* One way to do this is with a separate notebook divided into alphabetical sections; another is to keep a notebook by subject. Encourage students to list the meaning of each word in English and their native language. Some students may also benefit by including a small drawing of the concept of the word next to it.

Extension

Encourage students to get a more complete map of the Colorado River to follow as they read about the journey Powell and his crew took. Students can use either the map in the book or a larger map and match locations in the article to locations on the map. Students may also want to examine a topographical map to gain more information about the terrain through which the river flows.

Internet Connection

http://www.azstarnet.com/grandcanyonriver/ GCrt.html
Students can "run" the Colorado River through the Grand Canyon. The site highlights landmarks that students can click on to join the run. Students watch a QuickTime® movie of a small boat running Lava Falls Rapid by clicking on "Havasu Creek to Lava Falls."

Vocabulary Strategies Notes

The Student Edition of the *Reading Strategies* series includes vocabulary exercises to help students learn how to understand the meaning of unknown words. When students are puzzled during reading because they do not know specific words, the process of comprehension may be halted. Often, students find it discouraging and difficult to continue reading. The exercises offer specific methods students can use to understand unknown words.

Using the Vocabulary Excercises

You may want to use these exercises to help students comprehend their reading. You may also choose to use them as isolated exercises. For example, if you have noticed that students have trouble understanding the meaning of a word using prefixes and suffixes, you may want to assign that exercise to a student or to the class as a whole.

Practice Suggestions

Once students complete these exercises, they should reinforce their learning with practice. Perhaps most helpful is practice with the reading students normally do for classes. Suggest that students either form small groups or work individually to read a selection from a textbook or other assigned reading. As they read, ask students to look for examples of the kind of words mentioned in a particular vocabulary exercise. Students can list the words and determine their meanings using the techniques in the exercise.

The Exercises

These exercises have been chosen because they provide direct help with figuring out the meaning of difficult words. Here is an overview of what the exercises are intended to accomplish.

Exercise 1 (pages 91–92)
Words with Multiple Meanings

These words can often prove puzzling to students, particularly in different content areas. For example, a word such as *factor* has one meaning in math and has a different but somewhat related meaning in social studies. This exercise teaches students techniques for dealing with these multiple-meaning words.

Exercise 2 (page 93)
Context Clues: Part I

Included in this exercise are explicit directions for several approaches to using context. Students learn how to look for information about the meaning of words in surrounding words and sentences and how to seek other usages of unknown words that help provide a wider base of information.

Exercise 3 (pages 94–95)
Context Clues: Part II

Often, unknown words can be understood by looking not just at the general context in which they appear but also at the specific clues that authors provide. These may include definitions after words, restatement, meaning through example, and meaning through comparison and contrast.

Exercise 4 (pages 96–97)
Signal Words

Active readers can find clues to meaning through signal words. These words can alert readers to the introduction of new information, including a new subject, a series of steps, or a restatement of the author's main point. As students learn what words to look for and what each signals, they will become more proficient readers.

Apply What You Have Learned

The selections in the final review section of the Student Edition give students an opportunity to apply the reading strategies used in the text. To help students implement the strategies on their own, review the following guidelines with them.

Preview Guidelines

• Write the selection title.

• List the subheadings.

• Write any information that the title and subheadings tell about what you will read.

• Write what you know about the topic.

• Look at any photos, charts, and maps in the selection. You should read the captions carefully, too.

As students continue their preview of the selection, have them answer the following questions.

• What do the first and last paragraphs tell you about the topic?

• What do the topic sentences tell you about the topic?

• How is the text organized?

• What do you think you will learn from your reading?

Guidelines for Taking Notes

Once students have completed their preview of a selection, work with them to choose an appropriate strategy and graphic organizer. Remind students that they can review all the strategies on the inside back cover of their book before they make a choice. Also remind students that they should read first, then take notes. Taking notes while reading can cause students to lose their place and their train of thought. If students need to refresh their memory about details in the selection, they can reread.

When they have finished taking their notes, remind students to review their work. This last review will ensure that students have understood their readings.

Assessment Guidelines

The following graphic demonstates how the SQ3R strategy might work for the selection "The Battle of Belleau Wood." You might use this sample to help you assess students' graphic organizers. Notice that this student has used questions and notes to construct a coherent summary of the selection.

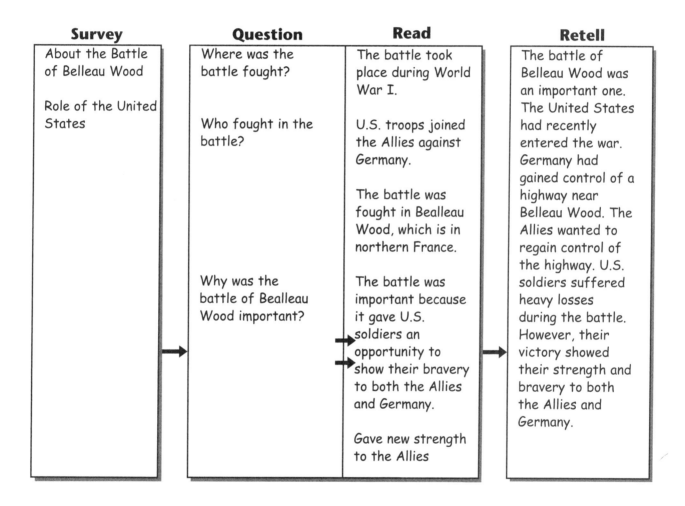

Survey

About the Battle of Belleau Wood

Role of the United States

Question

Where was the battle fought?

Who fought in the battle?

Why was the battle of Bealleau Wood important?

Read

The battle took place during World War I.

U.S. troops joined the Allies against Germany.

The battle was fought in Bealleau Wood, which is in northern France.

The battle was important because it gave U.S. soldiers an opportunity to show their bravery to both the Allies and Germany.

Gave new strength to the Allies

Retell

The battle of Belleau Wood was an important one. The United States had recently entered the war. Germany had gained control of a highway near Belleau Wood. The Allies wanted to regain control of the highway. U.S. soldiers suffered heavy losses during the battle. However, their victory showed their strength and bravery to both the Allies and Germany.

Reading Assessment

Effective readers tend to score well on state and standardized reading tests. You can also monitor, or have students monitor, their progress by using alternative forms of assessment. Here are some ways to gauge how well students understand and retain what they read:

Written Assessment

- **Portfolios** Student portfolios have gained in popularity because they enable a student to showcase the work he or she is proudest of. Self-selected student work can show a student's increasing ability in reading. Students might file a copy of their notes, a graphic organizer, and a summary for selection.

- **Journals** Students can keep a journal in which they record reflections on their reading, vocabulary, and strategy use. Reviewing students' journals periodically and discussing them as time permits will help you assess students' understanding. Caution students that they should include in their journal only information they want to share.

- **Self-Assessment** Students generally are aware of their own strengths and weaknesses. Allowing them to use this knowledge can improve student comprehension and confidence. Discuss students' observations about their work. This can be done in weekly sessions as students complete a reading selection. Work on a plan both to acknowledge students' successes and to address their perceived weaknesses. This plan should focus on one or two weaknesses so that students will see progress.

Conferencing Assessment

- **Observations** Observing students' reading behaviors will provide additional insights into their ability to read strategically. Record your observations for each student. You might also wish to keep observation folders for all students to show their progress over time. Discuss your observations with students.

- **Interview Think-Alouds** Students who are having reading difficulties can benefit from an interview think-aloud. Ask a student to read a selection and, while reading, to explain what he or she is doing and thinking to understand the selection. Take notes while the student thinks aloud so that you do not have to interrupt the flow of the student's thoughts. Listen for an understanding of how the student previews; identifies the text structure, main points, and supporting details; and reviews the reading. Discuss effective and ineffective techniques with students. Once you have identified an area of difficulty, it will be easier to make a plan for improvement.

Reading Strategies and Test Preparation

In addition to helping students improve their comprehension of classroom assignments, the *Reading Stategies* series can also help students succeed on tests. The Apply It section in each selection helps students practice using reading strategies to check their comprehension. The Test Tips in these sections also offer students clues to understanding and correctly answering test questions. In addition, the Unit Reviews present reading selections and questions that can be used for review or as a test.

Preparing for Classroom Tests

Emphasize to students that when they use reading strategies, they will have done much of the work they need to do to prepare for tests. Display a completed graphic organizer and summary done by a student volunteer or by the class as a whole-class exercise.

Tell students that when it is time to prepare for a test, they can use their notes in two ways. First, they can review the notes. Second, they can write another summary based on the notes, and compare it with the first summary they wrote. That comparison will help students review the main points of the reading. Because they already have written the main points and details of the reading, the review can concentrate on these facts, not on a range of unorganized notes or dimly remembered details.

Using Reading Strategies on a Standardized Test

Suggest to students that reading strategies are equally useful on the reading comprehension sections of standardized tests. Students should first preview the reading and the test questions, read carefully, take notes (if it is allowed during the test), and then think about what they have read. Approaching reading in this systematic way will help students answer the comprehension questions that follow a reading.

Practice Tests in the Student Edition

In the Student Edition, each unit concludes with a Unit Review that is designed to serve as an assessment tool. These reviews can be used both to assess students' understanding of the strategies and to help them prepare for a standardized test. Each review includes a test that measures students' ability on both multiple-choice and short-answer questions. You might want to use a Unit Review to model how a student taking a reading comprehension test can approach a reading selection.

Test Tips

The Apply It sections in the units of the Student Edition contain tips for successfully answering test questions. These Test Tips will help students on both classroom and standardized tests.

Some Tips deal with multiple-choice questions and offer hints on understanding the question being asked. Other Test Tips discuss answering short-answer and essay questions. For example, students are told that when a question asks them to choose the main idea of a selection, some of the answers may contain correct information, but only one choice is the *main idea*.

Many Test Tips, even if they are directed toward one type of question, have general applicability. For example, a tip that applies to understanding the direction line *make an inference* applies to both multiple-choice and short-answer questions.

The *Reading Strategies* series offers flexibility in test preparation. It can help students review for classroom tests and succeed on standardized tests.

Using the Graphic Organizers

On the following reproducible pages are graphic organizers that are designed to be used in teaching the lessons or in reinforcing the ways students understand text. You may want to use these graphics as guides when making larger copies on the board or on a large piece of chart paper. You may also use them to make transparencies for use with an overhead projector or for copies for individual students.

Students who are visual learners may enjoy creating new forms of graphic organizers. Consider asking students to present designs of original graphic organizers to the class. Have them explain how these graphics work and how they help them understand the reading.

You can readily assess students' understanding of a selection by reviewing their graphic organizer. The organizers will give you a clear picture of what students have identified as the major points and supporting details of each selection. They will also show you how skillfully students preview and set questions for themselves that they then answer through reading.

Encourage students to keep their graphic organizers and any notes or summaries that they create. These devices will help them review for a test or build a reading portfolio.

Outline (page T41)

Besides using this graphic to teach the Outlining strategy, you can also use it to teach writing. You can demonstrate both how to outline an already written selection and how to use the outlining form as an aid to planning writing.

SQ3R Chart (page T42)

The SQ3R graphic can be used to understand any reading in which there are many possible items to preview, such as illustrations, headings, captions, and so on. Students begin by writing their predictions. They then write questions about the selection, answer their questions and take notes about what they have read, and retell what they have learned. Their last step is to review to check their understanding.

PLAN: Venn Diagram (page T43)

This graphic works well when writing compares two or more things. If the writing compares more than two items, draw additional interlocking circles. The elements in common go in the center; the elements distinct to each go in the outside area of each circle.

PLAN: Wheel-and-Spoke Diagram (page T44)

This is one of the most common graphic organizers for writing and reading. The main idea belongs in the center circle. The outside circles highlight the major points made in the writing. Underneath each circle, students can record the details that support each point. Students may add outside circles as needed.

PLAN: Sequence Chart (page T45)

This graphic works well for writing that is organized by time. In each box students should record an important event, followed by the next box with the next important event. It can also be used to record a series of causes and effects.

PACA (page T46)

In this graphic, students first fill in their predictions. They use the small boxes to check off correct predictions that were either edited or added. They then write the information that supports the prediction in the Support boxes.

Tree Map (page T46)

Some students may be better able to understand the concept of main idea and details with this more linear structure. The main idea belongs on the center line; the supporting details belong on the branches leading from the center line.

Name _____   Date _____

OUTLINE

I. _____

  A. _____

    1. _____

    2. _____

  B. _____

    1. _____

    2. _____

      a. _____

      b. _____

      c. _____

II. _____

I used this strategy for: _____

Name _____   Date _____

SQ3R

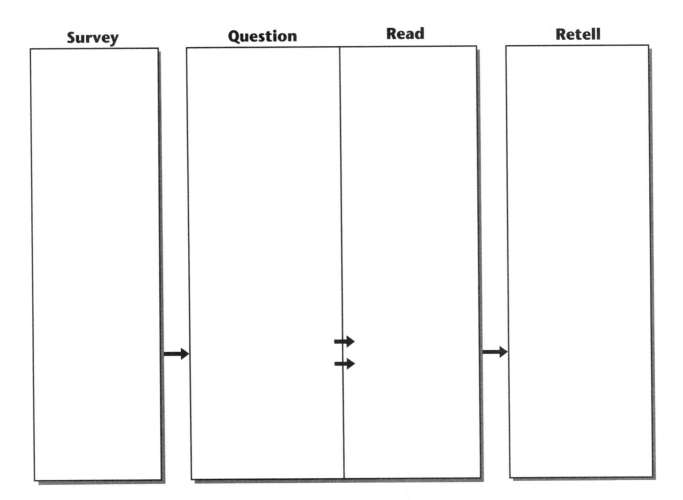

Survey   **Question**   **Read**   **Retell**

I used this strategy for: _____

Name _____   Date _____

PLAN: VENN DIAGRAM

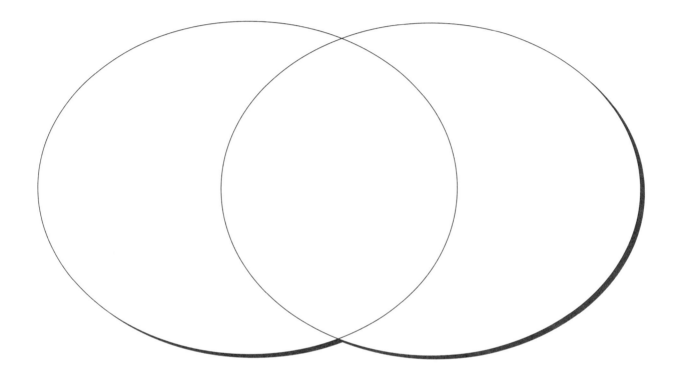

I used this strategy for: _____

Name _____   Date _____

PLAN: WHEEL-AND-SPOKE DIAGRAM

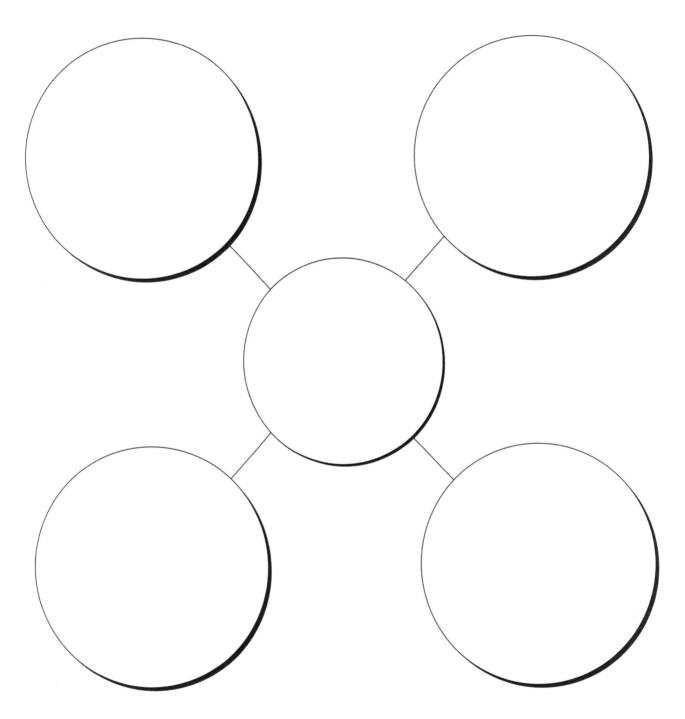

I used this strategy for: _____

Name _____   Date _____

PLAN: SEQUENCE CHART

I used this strategy for: _____

Name _____   Date _____

PACA

Prediction   **Support**

I used this strategy for: _____

Name _____   Date _____

TREE MAP

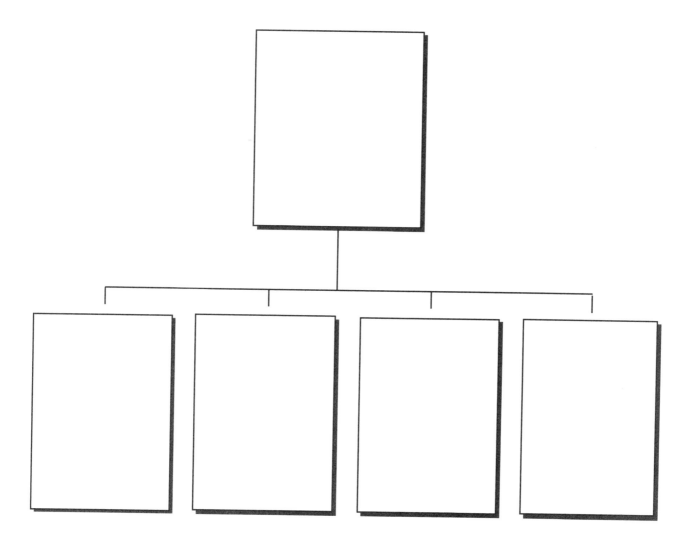

I used this strategy for: _____

Social Studies
Reading Strategies

Program Consultant
Dr. Kate Kinsella

San Francisco State University
San Francisco, California

Upper Saddle River, New Jersey
www.globefearon.com

Consultants

John Edwin Cowen, Ed. D.
Assistant Professor, Education/Reading;
Program Coordinator, Graduate M.A.T./
Elementary Education
School of Education
Fairleigh Dickinson University
Teaneck, NJ

Dr. Kate Kinsella
Dept. of Secondary Education and
Step to College Program
San Francisco State University
San Francisco, CA

Reviewers

Bettye J. Birden, M.A.
Reading Specialist
McReynolds Middle School
Houston, TX

Sally Parker, M.A.
T.R. Smedberg Middle School/
Sheldon High School
Elk Grove, Unified School District
Elk Grove, CA

Georgeanne Herbeck
District Supervisor, Elementary Education
Perth Amboy, NJ

Kenneth J. Ratti
Science Department Chairman
Vaca Peña Middle School
Vacaville, CA

Supervising Editor: Lynn W. Kloss
Senior Editor: Renée E. Beach
Editorial Assistant: Jennifer Watts
Writers: Sandra Widener, Terri Flynn-Nason
Production Editor: Laura Benford-Sullivan
Cover and Interior Design: Sharon Scannell
Electronic Page Production: Linda Bierniak, Phyllis Rosinsky, Wanda Rockwell
Manufacturing Supervisor: Mark Cirillo

Photo Credits
p. 8: The Museum of Modern Art/Film Still Archive; **p. 23:** Brown Brothers; **p. 29:** Photofest; **p. 32:** AP/Wide World; **p. 36:** Trevor Ray Hart-Katz/Matrix International, Inc.; **p. 45:** The Library of Congress; **p. 52:** UPI/Corbis-Bettmann; **p. 54:** The Library of Congress; **p. 71:** PhotoDisc, Inc.; **p. 74:** U.S. Army Photograph; **p. 82:** Archive photos; **p. 102:** Corbis-Bettmann; **p. 107:** Corbis-Bettmann

Printed in the United States of America   3 4 5 6 7 8 9 10   04 03 02 01
ISBN: 0-130-23798-1

1-800-848-9500
www.globefearon.com

Contents

To the Student

The Hows and Whys of Reading

Think of a story that you've read. Maybe it was about someone's exciting adventure. What did you want to know about the story? What kinds of questions did you ask to get that information?

If you were reading an adventure story, you probably wanted to know *who* the characters were and *when* and *where* they were going. These questions are very helpful when reading *literary text,* which includes things like short stories, novels, plays, and myths. They all tell a story.

There is another kind of writing that is called *informational text.* This kind of writing informs the reader by giving opinions, explanations, reasons,

Good Questions for Literary Text	Good Questions for Informational Text
who	how
when	what
where	why

facts, and examples about a certain topic. Things like chapters in a textbook and newspaper articles are considered informational text, so you are already familiar with this type of writing.

Think back to an example of literary text you've read. How are the questions you ask about a story different from the ones you ask when you read a chapter in your science book? In a science book, the questions *how*, *what*, and *why* are a great way to ask the "big" questions and get the information you are looking for. You might even start by changing the bold type headings and topic sentences into questions that begin with *how*, *what*, and *why*. Since *who, where* and *when* can be answered with a simple fact or one-word answer, they are not as useful when reading informational text. Look at the following example:

Heading		Question
Promoting Economic Growth	*becomes*	How can you promote economic growth?
Causes of Earthquakes	*becomes*	What causes earthquakes?
The Protests Affect U.S. Policy	*becomes*	Why do the protests affect U.S. policy?

These are examples of "big" questions. It is by asking these big questions that you will get the most out of the informational texts that you read. In this book, you'll learn more strategies for reading informational text and for remembering what you read.

Using Reading Strategies

Although you may not know it, you may already use a strategy when you read. Here's an example. You look at a magazine cover. A headline catches your eye. You see a picture of a musician or style of clothing you like. Then you look at the table of contents. Does an article sound interesting? If it does, you turn to that page. You look at a photograph in the article. Then you read the caption under it. You read the article. After you read, you think about what you have read. You have just used a reading strategy.

A reading strategy is a plan that helps you understand the information you read. The reading strategies in this book can help you understand your readings in social-studies textbooks. They can also help you understand things you read in your life outside of school or at a job. You will be able to link what you are reading to what you already know. Reading strategies will also help you remember what you read.

Becoming an Active Reader

When you use a strategy for reading, you take an active part in reading. You respond to the reading with thoughts, questions, and ideas. You also respond by taking notes or summarizing what you read. Finally, you think about what you read. What these steps have in common is that you are involved with what you are reading.

Steps of the Strategies

Although different strategies work well for different kinds of reading, all the strategies in this book have four steps in common. You preview. Then you read and take notes. Finally, you review. Below is a drawing of the steps of the reading strategies.

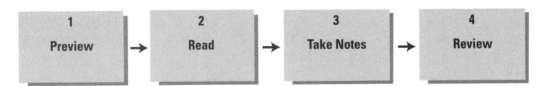

First, preview what you will read. In every strategy, you preview what you will read. When you preview, you think about what you already know about the topic. You also look for clues about what you will learn.

Here are the steps to use when you preview:

1. Look at the title. What clues does it give you about the topic?

2. Look at the illustrations or diagrams and read the captions. Often, major points are illustrated.

3. Read the first paragraph. It may include a summary of what is to come.

4. Read the last paragraph. It may sum up the writer's main points.

5. Read the first sentence of every paragraph. It will give you hints on what you will read.

Second, read carefully. As you read, think about what you are reading. What is the author telling you? Do you understand all of the words you are reading? Look for clues that the author has given you.

Third, take notes. The kind of notes you take will vary depending on what you are reading. A researcher found that students remember only 5 to 34 percent of the information they don't take notes on. When you take notes, you put information in your own words. That helps the information stay in your mind.

Fourth, review what you have read. You may review a section in a social studies textbook by comparing your notes on two countries you have read about. Often, though, you will want to write a summary. When you write a summary, you put the author's thoughts into your own words. You review the main points of the reading and the details that support these main points.

Choosing a Strategy

There are a variety of strategies in this book because people learn—and read—in different ways. After trying different strategies, you might find that one always works best for you. You may also find that one strategy works better on one type of reading. For example, one strategy might work well on an article on how to make a poster. Another strategy might work well on a debate about systems of government.

Experiment with these strategies. You'll find that you can use them on any reading you have, both in school and out of school. You'll also find that they'll help you make sense of your reading—and remember it!

Reading in Social Studies

You already read many kinds of social studies texts both in and out of school. You read history, geography, and government textbooks in school. At home you may read newspaper stories about news events. When you plan a vacation, you may read about the weather in your destination. You also may read to learn more about where you are going. Reading in social studies is a skill you will use often.

How Social Studies Reading Is Organized

Social studies consists of several subjects. These subjects include history, geography, and civics. Within these subjects you also may read about a culture or about economics. However, there are some patterns in the ways social studies readings are organized. When you recognize these patterns, you will better understand what you read because you'll be able to predict what will come next. Here are some common social studies patterns. You may see a combination of these patterns in one selection.

Main Idea and Details. This pattern in reading focuses on one main idea. Any social studies reading may be organized in this way. An article may explain a law. A history text may discuss a battle. When you see this organization, you know several points will explain or define the main idea.

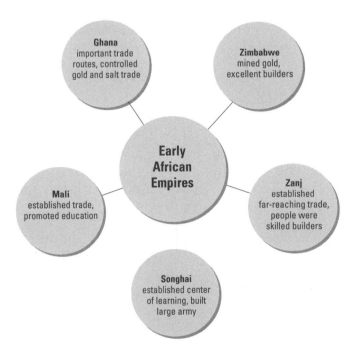

Compare and Contrast. Some reading requires you to think about how two things are alike and how they are different. For example, you may read about how two economic systems are similar. You may read about how two countries are different. When you see this pattern, you know the author wants you to think about what is alike and what is different about these topics. A Venn diagram like the one below can make the comparisons clear.

Athens and Sparta

Athens
wealthy,
democratic government,
strong trade,
colonies

Same
ancient Greek states

Sparta
military state,
ruled by small group of people,
wealth came from work or
enslaved people

Sequence of Events. You will often see this pattern in history texts. Events are presented in chronological, or time, order. Creating a timeline or a series of boxes can help you understand and keep track of this pattern. It also can help you see how one event led to another event.

The Civil War

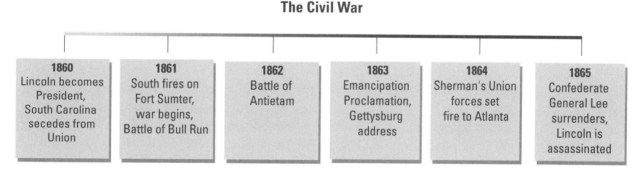

1860
Lincoln becomes
President,
South Carolina
secedes from
Union

1861
South fires on
Fort Sumter,
war begins,
Battle of Bull Run

1862
Battle of
Antietam

1863
Emancipation
Proclamation,
Gettysburg
address

1864
Sherman's Union
forces set
fire to Atlanta

1865
Confederate
General Lee
surrenders,
Lincoln is
assassinated

Getting the Most from Your Reading

If you can recognize the way a reading is organized, you will better understand what you read. You will be able to think about what kind of information might be next and how all the points in the reading fit together. Drawings like the ones on these two pages can show you these patterns. Thinking about how a reading is organized can help you understand—and remember—what you read.

Unit 1 Strategy: **Outlining**

Understand It......
Writing an outline can be a great way to create a study guide. When you take notes using an outline, you first preview to find the topic. You think of what you know about the topic, then you read. When you have finished reading, you review by making an outline. Use your outline to write a summary of the main points.

Try It..............
Read the article about the writer Sir Arthur Conan Doyle. He created a character you've probably heard of—Sherlock Holmes. Follow along with the student who has read the article and is creating an outline.

Step 1. Preview the selection.

Look at the title, the photograph, and the subheadings. Get an idea of the points the author is making. How is the article organized? You've probably read a few biographies either in school or on your own. You've seen that biographies can be organized in several ways. That is what the student thought as he skimmed the biography in this lesson.

The author could have written this biography in many ways. It could have been written chronologically—from Doyle's birth to his death. It could focus on one part of his life, such as the books he wrote. It could also show the events or people that shaped Doyle or his work. I can imagine other possibilities, too. Which organization is this? The subheadings might tell me.

Below, write what you can tell about the way the author organized the biography from previewing the article.

The article is in the order in which things happened in Doyle's life.

_____

_____

_____

Step 2. Read, then make an outline.

When most people make an outline, they use a formal style that may be familiar to you. It begins with Roman numerals for major ideas. Capital letters are used for major points that are part of each major idea. Numbers are used for supporting evidence for each major point. Titles and subheadings can help you find the major points and ideas in a piece of writing.

Here is how the student began outlining the article on the next two pages. After you read, add to the outline form to create a complete outline of the biography of Sir Arthur Conan Doyle.

Sir Arthur Conan Doyle

I. Early life
   A. From large family
   B. Studied to become a doctor
      1. Met Dr. Joseph Bell
      2. Learned to make deductions about patients
   C. Began to write novels
II. A Fork in the Road
   A. Became an eye doctor
      1. Wrote more Sherlock Holmes stories
      2. Got rid of Holmes character
      3. Revived Holmes character in 1904
   B. Became war reporter in Cairo, Egypt
III. The Later Years
   A. Wife died; Doyle remarried
   B. Invented new character
   C. Served in WWI

Sir Arthur Conan Doyle

Almost everyone knows the image. The thin man bent over a footprint is peering through a magnifying glass. Who else but Sherlock Holmes could be examining that footprint? Who else could solve the crime? The man who created Holmes was as interesting as his fictional character. Sir Arthur Conan Doyle lived a life of wide interests and great passions.

Early Life

Doyle was one of ten children. This was a large family even in the 1800s. Supporting so many children was a struggle. Doyle's uncles helped the family by sending Arthur to a Jesuit school. Although Doyle was a good student, he was unhappy.

Doyle went on to medical school. There he met a professor who made a big impact on his life. The professor, Dr. Joseph Bell, was known for his ability to make deductions about his patients. Doyle later put that skill to use in his writing. He had Sherlock Holmes make deductions about his cases.

Strategy Tip

Sometimes a new subheading signals that the author is introducing a new major idea.

Outlining

Sherlock Holmes and Watson

After graduation, Doyle served as a ship's doctor. He then entered practice with Dr. George Budd. Their partnership was not a happy one. In his spare time, Doyle did work he liked: writing. In 1887 his first work featuring Sherlock Holmes appeared. It was called *A Study in Scarlet.* During his time with Budd, Doyle kept writing. He published a long historical novel and then the Holmes mystery *The Sign of the Four.* In those years, Doyle's interests grew. He married Louise ("Touie") Hawkins in 1885.

A Fork in the Road

In 1890, Doyle needed a change. He went back to medical school to become an eye doctor. Because Doyle had few patients, he used his spare time to write. The Sherlock Holmes books remained popular. Holmes appeared in four novels and 56 stories. In 1893, Doyle grew tired of his creation. He killed off Holmes in a story titled "The Final Problem." There was a public **outcry**, but Doyle was unmoved. Then in 1905, he brought the detective back to life in *The Return of Sherlock Holmes.*

In the meantime, Doyle was ready for new adventures. He and his wife traveled to Cairo, Egypt. When a war started there, Doyle began a career as a war reporter.

The Later Years

When his wife died in 1906, Doyle became depressed. The following year, he married Jean Leckie, who had been a friend for years. Doyle then developed another character, Professor Challenger. In his time, Challenger became almost as famous as Holmes. When World War I broke out, Doyle formed a volunteer force. He also served as a war journalist.

Doyle's colorful life displays his energy and wide-ranging interests. His reputation today, though, rests on his fictional detective, Sherlock Holmes. The detective that Doyle tried to kill lives on and keeps Doyle's memory alive, too.

Step 3. Summarize what you have learned.

Look over your outline. Does it show you how the biography is organized and what the important points are? Add to your outline if you need to. Then use it to help you write a summary of the biography of Arthur Conan Doyle. Here is how the student began his summary of the biography:

Summary

Sir Arthur Conan Doyle was famous for his writing about Sherlock Holmes, but he did many other things in his life, too. His family was large and poor, but Doyle was able to go to medical school to become a doctor.

Then, though . . .

Now write your own summary of the biography on the lines below. Be sure to use your outline as you write to remind you of the major points and the evidence that supports them.

Sample answer: Sir Arthur Conan Doyle was famous for writing about Sherlock Holmes, but he did many other things in his life, too. His family was large and poor, but Doyle was able to go to medical school to become a doctor. He learned to make deductions about his patients. He had an unhappy partnership with a doctor, and began to write Sherlock Holmes stories. Although Doyle became an eye doctor, he kept writing Sherlock Holmes stories. At one point, he killed Holmes and then brought him back. Doyle also became a war reporter in Egypt. After his wife died, Doyle remarried, and invented a popular new character named Professor Challenger.

_____

_____

_____

_____

Apply It. . . . . Try outlining a reading assignment you have. First preview the assignment to see what the topic is. Notice the headings and subheadings. They will help you create your outline. Then draw the outline form on a separate piece of paper. Read the assignment, then create your outline. Remember to note the most important ideas on the Roman numeral lines.

When your outline is complete, use it to write a paragraph that summarizes your reading.

Lesson 1

Geography:
The Chocolate Journey

Understand It...... This geography selection tells how chocolate was brought from South America to Europe. The word *journey* in the title tells you that you might learn about a series of events. Outlining is a good strategy to use for selections that are organized in chronological, or time, order.

Try It............. Preview the selection, looking at the subheadings and the map. What do you notice about the way the selection is organized? On a separate piece of paper, create an outline after you read. Use the graphic below to remind you of the way an outline is set up.

```
I. _____
   A. _____
   B. _____
      1. _____
      2. _____
II. _____
   A. _____
   B. _____
      1. _____
      2. _____
```

The Chocolate Journey

Imagine this scene. A servant brings a cup of a new precious liquid into the room where the Spanish **nobles** are sitting. The nobles sniff. What is this? One lifts the cup to his lips. So began the passion for chocolate that gripped Spain in the 1500s, and later spread throughout Europe.

An Early American Favorite

Chocolate had long been a favorite drink in the Americas. Cacao trees originally grew in the river valleys of South America. In the seventh century, the Maya carried the trees and their seeds, cocoa beans, north into Mexico. The beans became so popular, they were used as money.

In 1502, Columbus made his fourth voyage to the Americas. He was the first explorer to take cocoa back to Spain. In 1519, a man who had sailed with the explorer and conqueror of Mexico, Hernán Cortés, tasted chocolate. Cortés's man saw Montezuma drink chocolate. The drink was served in golden cups, the explorer wrote. When he returned to Europe, Cortés's man told many people about this wonderful new drink.

The Columbian Exchange

The drink Cortés's man tried was not the cocoa we know. It had no sugar or milk. Instead, it was made with cocoa, red pepper, vanilla, and

Vocabulary Tip

What does *nobles* mean? You may be able to figure out the meaning from nearby words. Also think about the meaning of *noble* you already know.

READING STRATEGIES

OUTLINING

Strategy Tip

What does the map tell you about the Columbian Exchange? Add this information to your outline.

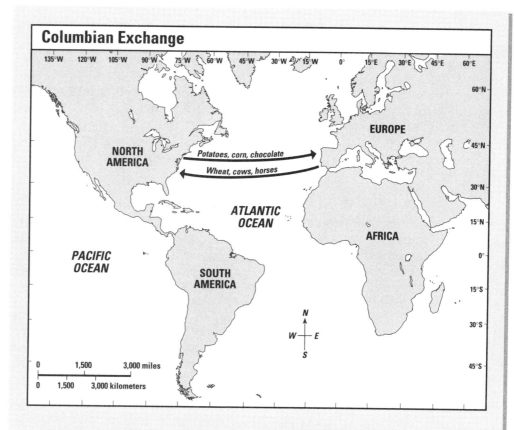

Columbian Exchange

water. Even so, cocoa made its way back to Europe. The movement of chocolate is part of the Columbian Exchange, which was named after Columbus. The Columbian Exchange was a network of trade Columbus began that linked the Americas and Europe. It developed as a result of the explorations of Columbus and many other explorers.

From the beginning of his journeys, Columbus took items he found in the Americas back to Europe. He loaded tomatoes, sweet potatoes, and pumpkins onto his ships. He carried squash and beans and tobacco and chocolate. When he returned to the Americas, Columbus brought horses, cows, and pigs from Europe. He also brought wheat and barley and sugar cane to the Americas.

The Columbian Exchange changed the world. The foods travelers found on their explorations began to be grown in Europe. The "new" foods spread to West Africa and China. Corn, potatoes, and beans became important foods for people all over the world. The discoveries of new food sources probably contributed to the global rise in population that began about then.

Chocolate's Popularity Grows

Once chocolate arrived in Europe, the people there began trying new things. They added sugar, cinnamon, cloves, and vanilla to the

Lesson 1   **11**

cocoa. The first factories to turn the beans into paste opened in Spain about 1580. Spain kept the secret for a few years. The drink had a great following among the nobility.

The secret of hot chocolate could not be kept for long. Outside Spain, people added only water, sugar, and vanilla to their cocoa. At first, the drink was sold in coffeehouses in London. Then fancy chocolate houses began to open. By the 1600s, the drink was a favorite of the upper classes in France and England. Within a few decades, hot chocolate was the rage of Europe.

The idea of adding milk to chocolate might have come from Jamaica. A doctor named Sir Hans Sloane lived there from 1687 to 1689. He saw young children being given a chocolate drink with milk in it. When Sloane returned to England, he told everyone about the drink. He became a big booster of hot chocolate with milk.

Chocolate Today

Europe became a world leader in the production of chocolate. A Dutch man invented a way to make cocoa powder. The first chocolate bar was made in 1819 in Switzerland. The manufacturer was Francois-Louis Cailler. In 1878, a writer remarked that chocolate candy was very popular. Today, chocolate remains many people's favorite. The many foods made from the bitter beans carried to Europe by Columbus still give pleasure to people all over the world.

Look over your outline. Does it include all the important information you learned while reading? If you need to, read again and revise your outline so that it gives a quick overview of the selection. When you finish your outline, you should have a good idea of how chocolate journeyed from the Old World to the New World.

Apply It . . . . To check your understanding of the selection, circle the best answer to each of the following questions.

1. Which of these statements is true?
   a. The cacao tree came originally from Mexico.
   b. Corn came from Europe.
   c. Wheat came from Europe.
   d. Cortés was the first explorer to take chocolate to Europe.

2. From his description of the way the cocoa was served, you can conclude that Cortés's man
   a. was eager to bring the beverage to Europe.
   b. thought Montezuma's court was wasteful.
   c. was impressed with the way it was served.
   d. wasn't interested in anything he saw.

3. The Columbian Exchange is named
    a. for the Columbians, who introduced chocolate to Europe.
    (b.) for Columbus, who began it.
    c. for Cortés, who began it.
    d. for Columbia, which was the first land Columbus visited.

4. You might conclude that chocolate was a favorite of the nobility in the 1500s because
    (a.) it was expensive, and only the rich could afford it.
    b. Columbus was a member of the nobility and introduced it to his friends.
    c. others were afraid to drink something from another country.
    d. poor people were not allowed to drink it.

5. The word *rage* in the second paragraph of the section "Chocolate's Popularity Grows" means
    a. anger.
    b. happiness.
    c. an unpopular thing.
    (d.) a very popular thing.

Test Tip

Unless the instructions tell you otherwise, always use complete sentences when you answer a short-answer question.

Use the lines below to write your answers for numbers 6 and 7. You can use the map in this lesson and your outline to help you.

6. Summarize chocolate's journey from the Americas to Europe. How did it reach Europe, and how did it become popular there?

Chocolate first came to Europe when Columbus brought it back from the Americas. It became popular as a drink when people in Europe began adding sugar and spices to it.

_____

_____

_____

7. Write a definition of the Columbian Exchange. Explain how people in Europe and the Americas might have benefited from it.

The Columbian Exchange was the exchange of products native to the Americas being introduced to Europe and other parts of the world and products native to Europe being introduced to the Americas and other parts of the world. People in both continents gained new food sources.

_____

_____

_____

Understand It...... This article begins with an explanation of a period of Chinese history called the "Cultural Revolution." After you learn what the Cultural Revolution was, you will read about how several people lived through those difficult days. Because the organization of the article is clear, you can use outlining to help you understand the main points.

Try It.............. Below is a drawing of the form an outline usually takes. Refer to it as you write your outline. Before you begin, though, preview the article to get an idea of what you will read. Look at the subheadings and topic sentences to get an idea of the main points to include in your outline. Then read the article. When you have finished reading, write these points on your outline.

Strategy Tip

Read the article first, then go back and outline it.

```
I. _____
   A. _____
   B. _____
      1. _____
      2. _____
II. _____
   A. _____
   B. _____
      1. _____
      2. _____
```

Vocabulary Tip

The first sentence uses *suspect* as a verb, meaning "to consider someone to be guilty." *Suspect* can also be used as a noun, meaning "someone who might be guilty of a crime." What might the adjective *suspect* mean?

The "Ten Years Disaster"

In 1949, after a long civil war, China became a Communist state. The first ruler was Mao Zedong, who governed until his death in 1976. In the mid-1960s, Mao decided that the revolution had weakened. Some of his advisers urged that China update its Communist policies. That updating led to the Cultural Revolution, which began in 1966 and lasted about ten years.

Mao decided that to keep the revolution alive, he would get rid of everyone he **suspected** of opposing his policies. This group included most of the "thinkers." Teachers and scientists were especially **suspect**. They were accused of not supporting the revolution strongly enough. After a while, even having the wrong background meant that people lost their jobs and were ridiculed. The wrong background might mean coming from a family that once had money or owned land.

Students were organized into what were called Red Guards. They were encouraged to turn in teachers and other students suspected of being politically "incorrect." The Red Guard became a force to fear. Its members attacked people whenever they wanted. At any time, a Red Guard could declare that a person was not a true Communist. Homes and stores were destroyed. People were injured and even killed. In addition to experiencing terror every day, an entire generation of Chinese people had little education.

It took years for the fear and the attacks to ease. By the mid-1970s, however, life had become a little more normal. Universities reopened. The government became more interested in increasing production and improving the lives of the Chinese people. The Cultural Revolution was over, but people remembered the time of terror.

A University Student

I knew we might be in trouble. My father was something of a free thinker. The Red Guard did not like that. Guards came for him one day at our home. They marched up the front walk and broke down the door.

I was a student then. I was studying, and my father was working. He heard them come and whispered to me to leave by the back door. "They don't want you!" he said. "They want me."

I was so frightened that I took his advice. Now I am ashamed. I heard the sound of breaking glass. The Red Guard smashed the bookcases on the floor. Then I saw them leave with my father. They made him wear a large sign. It said he admitted he was a wrong-headed intellectual. They paraded him through the streets like that.

Seeing my scholarly, quiet father treated that way hurt. From that moment, I never trusted the Cultural Revolution. We now call it the "Ten Years Disaster."

A Person from the "Wrong Background"

Because my family had some money, we were considered bad. I was not even allowed to join the Red Guard. I wanted desperately to prove that I was pure, so I signed up to go to the country. I wanted to learn from the poor and to re-educate myself.

That winter was impossibly hard. There was almost no food for the **peasants** who worked the land and less for students like us. I almost died of starvation.

Near the end of the time I was there, the wells dried up. The only water left was from the river. That was muddy, and we could not drink it. Unlike the **peasants** who lived there, we had some choices. We decided to run for home. We jumped on a train when no one was looking and went back to the city.

A Red Guard

I can tell you that what we did, we did for the country, at least at first. We wanted China to grow strong. Mao told us that unless we rid China of the bad elements—people who were not revolutionaries—China's great revolution would die. I deeply believed in what we were

Strategy Tip

Before you begin an outline, decide how a reading is organized. This article contains a collection of people's experiences. The best way to outline it is to start a new Roman-numeral line for each new person.

Vocabulary Tip

You can understand the meaning of the word *peasants* by looking at how it is used both times in this section.

Vocabulary Tip

Dashes often enclose information that explains or gives more details about the words near them.

World History:
The "Ten Years Disaster"

doing. We were helping the country stay strong! We were getting rid of the evil forces that kept China from moving ahead, the greedy business owners and the teachers who wanted to kill the people's revolution!

Looking back, I do feel some shame. I helped destroy the house of a man on our street who had always been kind to me. I do not think he ever even thought about politics. That's just the way it was back then.

A Child

We were young during the Cultural Revolution. I knew they had taken my father to a camp, which was at the local high school. We were supposed to be in school already, but the school was being used to house enemies of the revolution.

I left one day without telling my mother. I was afraid because I knew that the children of those who had been taken to camps were considered to be very bad, too. We were the enemy. There was a general feeling that whatever happened to us was fine because we were the children of bad people. They called us "puppy dogs."

I finally got to the camp. Two fierce men with guns guarded the gate. One of the men knew my father. He must have taken pity on me because when the other guard wasn't looking, he let me in. I saw my father. His head was bowed. His hands were behind his back. He was being walked across the yard. A man followed him, hitting my father with a rifle. I never forgot how sad and thin my father looked and how defeated he seemed. It made me feel frightened. I realized that my father could not protect me.

A Professor

I deeply believed in the revolution. Against my better judgment, I had even accused friends of being anti-revolutionary. I had felt justified, even proud, of my actions to get rid of professors I thought were not strong revolutionaries. I was considered a shining example of a quickly rising intellectual, one who was destined to run the universities.

Then I became a target. I had written a book that the party decided praised individuals too much. I needed to be "re-educated."

I was taken to a room. The walls were plastered with huge signs that **denounced** me and my work. I looked at my fellow professors. Some looked blank. Others, whom I had denounced in the past, looked faintly satisfied. So now I was to find out what it was like! It was horrible. People I had known for many years shook their fingers at me and yelled. It remains the most unsettling experience of my life.

Vocabulary Tip

Try to substitute another word to figure out the meaning of *denounced* in this paragraph.

After you read, create your outline. Be sure it tells what each person's experiences were during the Cultural Revolution. Then use your outline to write a summary of what you read. Be sure to include an explanation of what the Cultural Revolution was.

Apply It. . . . . To check your understanding of the article, circle the best answer to each question below.

1. Mao Zedong began the Cultural Revolution because
    a. he wanted to prove the Chinese people were loyal to him.
    (b.) he thought that the country's revolutionary spirit was weakening.
    c. he suspected that the workers were plotting against him.
    d. he wanted to prove that the Chinese people supported the revolution.

2. To join the Red Guards, a person had to be
    (a.) a student.
    b. an intellectual.
    c. a peasant.
    d. ready to enlist in the army.

3. The term *puppy dogs* refers to
    a. the young children of the Red Guards.
    b. those who kept studying after the schools closed.
    c. the younger brothers and sisters of Red Guard members.
    (d.) the children of those who were thought to be anti-revolutionaries.

4. In the last paragraph, the word *denounced* means
    (a) spoken against.
    b. known.
    c. spoken about.
    d. helped.

5. You can conclude that the Red Guard who helped destroy a man's house now feels that the Cultural Revolution
    a. was a complete success.
    b. is the reason China's economy is growing today.
    c. was a complete failure.
    (d.) might have gone too far.

Use the lines below to write your answers for numbers 6 and 7. Use your outline to help you.

6. Who was in danger of being a target during the Cultural Revolution? How were these people alike?

People in danger of being targeted during the Cultural Revolution were the intellectuals, scientists, and thinkers. People from the "wrong backgrounds"—people with money—or those suspected of being enemies of Mao's policies were also in danger.

Test Tip

Question 7 asks you for *effects*. Look for details from the article that explain what happened in China *as a result* of the Cultural Revolution.

7. What were the effects of the Cultural Revolution in China?

A whole generation had little or no education, people were terrorized and attacked for little reason, and houses and stores were destroyed.

Lesson 3

Economics: Ecotourism: Savior or Destroyer?

Understand It...... This article discusses a trend in tourism: ecotourism. You might not have heard of ecotourism, but you've heard of tourism. If you have ever explored a new place, you have been a tourist.

Try It.............. Preview the article to get a clearer idea of what you will be reading. By looking at the subheadings, you can see that the article discusses the good and bad points of ecotourism. As you prepare your outline, you might write each subheading on a separate capital-letter line. List supporting details on the number lines underneath each one.

Strategy Tip

When you preview, think about what you know about tourism. You've probably been a tourist. You also may have seen tourists visiting *your* town.

```
I. _____
   A. _____
   B. _____
      1. _____
      2. _____
II. _____
   A. _____
   B. _____
      1. _____
      2. _____
```

Vocabulary Tip

Divide *ecotourism* into parts to figure out its meaning. The base word *tourism*, means "traveling for pleasure." The prefix *eco-* is a shortened form of *ecology*, the science of the environment. Put these word parts together to define *ecotourism*.

Ecotourism: Savior or Destroyer?

An animal rustles in the thick jungle. The native guide puts a finger to his lips. A rare bird reappears, flashing its red tail. The tourists smile at one another and head back to the lodge. When they arrive, the staff serves a delicious meal. The staff consists mainly of local people. The cook used foods from the jungle. The gift shop sells local crafts.

That's the image supporters of **ecotourism** like. They think of ecotourism as responsible travel to natural areas. The movement began in the mid-1980s. That was when tourism became important in the world.

From 1950 to 1988, the number of vacationers who traveled to another country rose from about 25 million to about 400 million. By the year 2000, tourism is expected to be the world's largest industry.

Ecotourism began as a small part of that growth. Some tourists wanted to learn about people and places. They wanted to visit wild areas and see wildlife. In the 1980s, ecotourism became more common.

Some visitors wanted more. They wanted to make sure their visit didn't ruin a natural place. They wanted some of their money to go to the people whose land they were visiting. The idea of ecotourism spread.

Strategy Tip

The subheadings on this page tell you that you'll be reading about different opinions on ecotourism.

Vocabulary Tip

The word *impact* can be a verb that means "to hit" or a noun that means "an effect." You can tell by the sentence which meaning fits here.

Savior?

Ecotourism has many benefits, its supporters say. Ecotourists often visit areas where people are poor. They bring in needed money. Native people can stay in their communities and work. Supporters say that ecotourism can help preserve local arts.

Supporters also say that ecotourists care about the environment. They don't need superhighways built through a jungle. Ecotourists travel on local roads. They prefer simple cottages to giant hotels with swimming pools.

Many people argue that ecotourism can help people of different cultures understand one another. When tourists go to a huge, fenced-in resort, they have a harder time getting to know the place or the people. For ecotourists, the point of the trip is learning about the local culture.

Destroyer?

Ecotourism does have its enemies, though. They argue that ecotourism can affect people and places more than a huge resort does. Huge resorts, critics say, can't change the local people.

They say that ecotourism can damage the environment, too. Often, ecotourists travel to fragile areas. Tourists to such places will have some sort of **impact**, critics say. They can easily damage these places.

Critics worry that ecotourism means taking advantage of local artists. They say that important cultural items can become toys for tourists. Some also say that local people can lose control of their land.

Ecotourism at Work

The ecotourism movement has had some successes and some failures. In Panama, the Kuna Indians have a wildlife preserve on their land. They tried to attract ecotourists. Bad roads and few connections with travel agents helped defeat their project. Costa Ricans who lived near a popular national park also tried to form businesses to attract tourists. They didn't succeed. They couldn't compete with outsiders who had the money to build.

In Ecuador, the Quichua people decided to encourage ecotourism. A community called Capirona built several tourist cottages in the traditional style. The people used thatch and bamboo. Visitors take guided walks through the forest. They eat Quichua meals. They learn about the culture of the Quichua. Tourists use a blowgun. They learn how to make an animal trap. They even perform songs or dances after the Quichua teach them their dances and songs. Money the visitors spend goes to the community.

Whether critics like it or not, ecotourism is growing. Some tourist groups have set guidelines for ecotourism. The most important one is that ecotourism must involve the local people. They have the most to lose. If ecotourism is successful, they also have the most to gain.

Economics:
Ecotourism: Savior or Destroyer?

Look over your outline to make sure that it shows all major points mentioned in the article. Then use your outline to write a summary of what you have read. Your summary will help you review the article.

Apply It........... To check your understanding of the article, circle the best answer to each question below.

1. The main point of this article is that
    a. ecotourism can be good for the local people.
    b. ecotourism is as bad as regular tourism for the environment.
    c. ecotourism has supporters and critics, but it is popular now.
    d. ecotourism is on the rise.

Test Tip

In question 2, you are asked to choose which answer is *not* a criticism. That means the other answers *are* criticisms.

2. Which of these is *not* a criticism of ecotourism?
    a. Ecotourists can destroy fragile environments.
    b. Ecotourists don't spend as much money as regular tourists do.
    c. Ecotourism can affect local people more than a huge resort might.
    d. Ecotourism can turn local arts into toys for tourists.

3. What can you infer about the destinations of ecotourists?
    a. They are in Europe.
    b. They are very popular.
    c. They are in parts of the world not many people have visited.
    d. They are good places for outside builders.

4. What is the difference between tourists and ecotourists?
    a. Only ecotourists travel to natural areas.
    b. There is no difference.
    c. Tourists spend more money in the areas they visit.
    d. Only tourists buy crafts from the native people.

Test Tip

Question 5 asks you for the *main* reason some ecotourism locations succeed. Some of these choices may be correct, but only one is the *main* reason.

5. What is the most important guideline for ecotourism?
    a. The builders must have enough money to build hotels.
    b. The resorts must not harm the environment.
    c. The area must be beautiful and have a lot of wildlife.
    d. The local people must be involved.

Use the lines below to write your answers for numbers 6 and 7. Your outline and your summary will help you.

6. What is ecotourism? Use details in the article to explain your definition.

Ecotourism is traveling to natural places to experience people and places unaffected by modern civilization.

7. Do you think ecotourism is a savior or a destroyer? Explain your choice.

Ecotourism can be a savior because it provides local people with jobs, which improves local economies; preserves local arts; and helps preserve the environment. Ecotourism can be a destroyer because it can damage the environment, exploit local artists, and take the control of resources away from local people.

Lesson 4

Civics: Should Women Vote?

Understand It...... This selection is about the debate over whether women should have the right to vote. People throughout the country argued about the issue in the late 1800s and early 1900s. In 1919, the 19th Amendment to the Constitution gave women the right to vote. You probably know something about women's struggle to vote. Using an outline will help you understand the debate.

Try It............. The speeches below were given by women around 1900. From the title, you know you will probably be reading a debate. People will present opposing opinions. You can also guess that the speeches will probably not be about the history of the issue. Each speaker will probably try to convince listeners that her opinion is correct. Preview the article for clues about what you will read. Then start reading. When you have finished reading, go back and outline the article. Use the outline below as a guide.

Strategy Tip

If you prefer, you can read the article first. Then go back and create an outline. The best way to create an outline is to read first and then to outline while you reread.

```
I. _____
   A. _____
   B. _____
      1. _____
      2. _____
II. _____
   A. _____
   B. _____
      1. _____
      2. _____
```

Vocabulary Tip

Suffragists are people who believe in women's *suffrage*, or women's right to vote.

Should Women Vote?

Taken from records at the New York Century Club, 1901

AGAINST: Mrs. Julia M. Shaw

Gentlemen: I stand before you today, a woman proud to be a homemaker, a wife, and a mother. I fill my days serving those I love. I think only of their welfare. I am distressed at the **suffragists** who would force upon me a radical change in the way society sees me and in the way I see the world. Allow me to explain why I firmly believe that our current system—which has served us well for hundreds of years—should stand.

Women are not meant for the affairs of the world. We are meant to deal with the affairs of the heart and of the home. That is where our interest is and where our interest should be. I have no desire to change places with my husband and wear his trousers. I wish to devote my time and energy to the affairs that matter to me. If I were to devote my time

Civics:
Should Women Vote?

instead to the affairs of state that concern him, my attention would be diverted. That would not be good for my family or for me. On a larger scale, such a diversion of women's attention would not be good for the nation. Women have always been devoted to the home, not to the greater affairs outside the home. If we direct our attention outside the home, our families will suffer as will the entire structure of society.

What is more, I do not have the information to make the decisions voting would thrust upon me. I do not spend my days reading great tomes, nor do I spend my days in deep discussion of world affairs. How am I to know the correct vote? Far better to leave that to the husbands of the world, who are willing to **shoulder that burden** for us women. They are equipped for it. We are not.

I also would hesitate to vote knowing that I could send men to war to die but could not go myself. War is men's work. However, if women were granted the right to vote, they would be voting to direct others to go to wars on foreign ground and die for them. That right, if one wishes to call it that, is not one I would choose to exercise.

Why force the vote on a population that has no desire to have it? In Massachusetts in 1895, women were asked if they wanted the vote. Only 5 percent said yes. Women don't want change.

These suffragettes who claim to represent us do not. They are women who bully, women who are unladylike. They are bitter women who are outside the mainstream of society and who apparently want to be men.

In Kansas in 1887, women were given the right to vote on local issues. Since then, the vote for women has not been extended. Women still cannot vote in other elections. If women's suffrage works, why have these rights not been further extended? The answer is that voting by women does not work well, and women *do not want this right!*

Allow us to return to the gracious days when women were able to live the lives they were intended to live. We do not want to be men. We want to be women. Allow us that right.

FOR: Mrs. Charlotte Ramsey

Women suffragettes are no more than true daughters of the Revolution. We believe what our founders believed in and the principles for which they fought and died. We believe in equality. We believe that women, as much as men, have the right to make decisions about their government.

Why should we not have this right? We are thinking, breathing, intelligent people. What is strange about the current debate is who the anti-suffragist movement believes should vote and who should not. Our schoolteachers are mostly women. Yet such women, many of them

Vocabulary Tip

You can understand the phrase *shoulder that burden* by looking both at the context and at the words in the phrase. If you *shoulder* something, you put it on your shoulder or carry it. The writer is saying that men are willing to take on that burden, or task.

Strategy Tip

Be sure to include outline entries for both speeches.

college educated, are not considered the intellectual equals of men who can neither read nor write, men who might have had no more than a year or two of school. I ask you, who is the better decision maker likely to be?

Women demonstrate (in a march through New York City) in 1912 for the right to vote.

We women who ask for the vote are like our Revolutionary brothers in another way. We do not believe in taxation without representation. That is exactly what is happening today. Many women, both married and single, own property and pay taxes on it. Yet those women have no say in the taxes they must pay. That issue led to the Revolutionary War. We do not intend to fight, but we do intend to seek the one thing that can change this disgraceful situation. We want to vote.

Women must also obey laws they do not agree with but that govern them. Times have changed. Not all women have the protection of a man or a family. They take care of themselves. Laws designed to protect women, laws that govern the jobs they may hold, are based on the idea that every woman has the protection and economic support of a man. Women who must depend on themselves often suffer.

Some people say women are not **fit** to vote because they live in the shelter of the home and have no experience of the world. That is not true now, if it ever was. Women graduate from college, they read, and they think. Many work and earn money. They certainly have the knowledge and desire to participate in the country's life. Women are fit to be partners in the enterprise of government.

Women are more than just fit partners in government; they are essential partners. Women's point of view should be part of the discussion. Women plan for the future of children. They understand domestic issues in ways that men cannot. Women might be hesitant to send our sons to war—but is that the position of a weaker sex or the position of a sex responsible for the good health of its offspring? Perhaps if women had voted, some needless wars might have been avoided. Women offer a perspective critical to balanced public debate.

Women should have the vote. We—and the country—deserve no less!

Vocabulary Tip

You probably know a few definitions for *fit.* You know that when a shirt *fits*, it's the right size. You may also know another meaning for fit; "to be qualified for." Which meaning makes sense here?

After you have finished reading, create your outline. Make sure you included all the important points of both speakers. Use your outline to write a summary that will help you remember what you read.

Civics:
Should Women Vote?

Apply It......... To check your understanding of the debate, circle the best answer to each question.

1. Which argument does Mrs. Shaw make against women's suffrage?
   a. Women do not have the information to vote.
   b. Women are too emotional to vote.
   c. Women are not meant to deal with affairs of state.
   d. all of the above

2. When Mrs. Shaw says that she does not want to wear her husband's trousers, she means
   a. she wants to wear frilly dresses.
   b. she does not want her husband to feel less important.
   c. people will think she is a suffragist if she wears his trousers.
   d. she does not want to take on what she thinks of as a male role.

3. "I do not spend my days reading great tomes, nor do I spend my days in deep discussion of world affairs." In this sentence, the word *tomes* means
   a. remarks.
   b. ideas.
   c. books.
   d. maps.

4. You can infer that Mrs. Ramsey mentioned the American Revolution because
   a. she wanted to connect the Revolution and women's suffrage.
   b. she wanted men to feel ashamed that women could not vote.
   c. she wanted her listeners to feel patriotic.
   d. she knew there would be veterans in the audience.

5. The two speakers differ on the issue of
   a. whether women are smart enough to vote.
   b. whether women should be married.
   c. whether women want to be involved in national affairs.
   d. whether women should have children.

6. Continued...
such decisions as sending men to war, when they cannot fight themselves. Women have no interest in voting and no desire to vote. Arguments for: Women suffragettes, like the founders of the country, want to be represented. They want equality and, like the revolutionaries, they do not want taxation without representation. Women are as able to make decisions as men are but must live by laws they did not make. Women are essential partners in government because of the female perspective they offer.

Use the lines below to write your answers for numbers 6 and 7. Use your outline notes to help you.

6. Write a few sentences that describe this debate.

Sample answers: Arguments against: Women are not meant for the affairs of the world. Being involved in worldly affairs would take women away from the home, which is a woman's place. Women do not have the information to make decisions about the world, nor should they make

...continued

7. How do you think having the right to vote could change the way a person thinks about himself or herself?

Sample answer: The right to vote allows people to voice their opinions. When people vote, they choose their best option. If they vote for a significant change and that change is made, those people will gain a great sense of accomplishment. People want to know that their beliefs and opinions are considered.

Test Tip

You should already have a good summary you can use to help you answer question 6.

Unit *1* Review: **Outlining**

In this unit, you have practiced using the outlining reading strategy. Use this strategy when you read the selection below. Use a separate sheet of paper to create an outline, take notes and summarize what you learn.

Hint *Remember that all reading strategies have activities for before, during, and after reading. To review these steps, look at the inside back cover of this book.*

America's Most Famous Traitor

Benedict Arnold became famous for betraying his country. His name came to mean "traitor." At the start of the Revolutionary War, though, Benedict Arnold was a hero. Why did he betray his country?

Benedict Arnold was born in Connecticut. His family was well respected. During the French and Indian War, from 1754 to 1763, he fought in the colonial army.

After his father died, in 1761, Arnold moved back home. He became a druggist and bookseller. In 1775, as the American colonies prepared to fight for independence, Arnold was elected captain of an army unit.

Arnold was in the middle of the fight for independence from the start. He helped lead the charge to take Fort Ticonderoga from the British in 1775. George Washington's troops were able to use the supplies from that fort to stay alive. That same year, Arnold led a charge on British Quebec. The attack failed. Even so, Arnold was promoted to brigadier general.

In 1777, Benedict Arnold led the attack in the Battle of Ridgefield, Connecticut. He gained fame for his courage. Then Arnold became commander of Philadelphia in 1778. There he met Margaret Shippen. They soon married. The couple spent money freely.

Next, Arnold became head of West Point, a critical post. West Point protected the Hudson Valley.

Then Arnold did something no one expected. He offered to give West Point to the British for money.

On the night of September 23, 1780, three colonial soldiers captured a British major named John Andre. He was carrying papers that told of Arnold's plot. Andre was hanged as a spy. Arnold learned of Andre's capture and fled to a British warship in the Hudson River. The British made him an officer in their army.

The Trail of the Traitor

Why did Benedict Arnold do it? One reason was money. Arnold and

Unit 1 Review: Outlining

his wife did not have the money to support their rich tastes. Also, Arnold was angry because younger officers were promoted above him.

The army in Philadelphia also claimed that Arnold ignored military law. Those charges made him furious. All these factors built up. Finally, Arnold decided to betray his country.

After his escape, Arnold fought against the colonies. In his home state, Connecticut, Arnold burned more than 150 buildings. His British troops killed colonial soldiers.

Finally, in 1781, Arnold and his family left America for Britain. The British saw him as a traitor. If he would betray his country once, they thought, he would do it again.

Arnold was less successful in business in England than he had been in the colonies. The deal he had made was more costly than he had expected.

Use your outline and summary to help you answer the questions below.

1. Which of the following did Benedict Arnold do?
   a. He helped George Washington lead the army.
   b. He hanged John Andre.
   c. He betrayed his country to the British.
   d. He became a respected British citizen.

2. Why was West Point important in the Revolutionary War?
   a. It was an important center for communications.
   b. It protected the Hudson Valley.
   c. It was the training ground for colonial officers.
   d. It was the British headquarters.

3. Arnold was distrusted by the British because
   a. they considered him to be an American at heart.
   b. they didn't trust someone who had betrayed his country.
   c. he was not useful to the British once he left America.
   d. he never became a British citizen.

4. Why was Andre's capture important to the colonial forces?

Andre was a spy. When the Americans captured him, he was carrying papers that described Arnold's plot.

5. Why did Benedict Arnold betray his country?

One reason Arnold betrayed his country was money. He was also angered by the charges that he ignored military law.

Unit 2 Strategy: **SQ3R**

Understand It...... SQ3R is short for **S**urvey, **Q**uestion, **R**ead, **R**etell, and **R**eview. This reading strategy will help you focus your thoughts before you read. Focusing your thoughts helps you prepare to learn new information. It helps you look for information while you read. Finally, it helps you remember what you learn.

Try It.............. The movie review in this lesson discusses the re-release of *Star Wars* 20 years after it first appeared in movie theaters. Read the steps a student followed as she used the SQ3R strategy to think about and understand the review. Then work along with her to learn the strategy yourself.

Step 1. Survey what you will read.

Before you read, survey, or preview, the movie review. Look quickly at the text and ask yourself what it is about. Look at the title, subheadings, the first and last sentences of each paragraph, and the topic sentences. Get an idea of what the writer wanted to say. Also, look at the pictures, maps, charts, and captions. All these things give you hints about what you will read.

Now survey the movie review starting on the next page. Then follow along with the student as she used the SQ3R strategy to understand it. As she surveyed, this is what she thought:

This review is about the re-release of the movie Star Wars. *The first subheading seems to ask if the movie is as enjoyable as it was when it was first made.*

The student then wrote these notes in her SQ3R chart. Add a few notes of your own to the chart after you complete your survey.

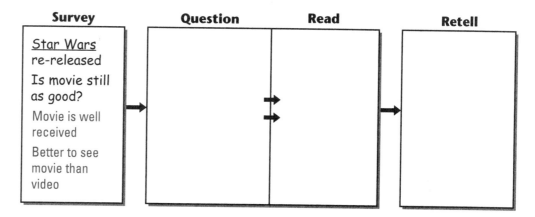

Step 2. Ask questions about what you might read.

After you survey, think of questions you have about the writing. For a review of *Star Wars*, you might ask yourself, "What do I know about the movie?" or "Do I agree with this reviewer? Does he or she make good points?" You can turn subheadings into questions, too. The student wrote this question in her SQ3R chart. Add your own questions about the movie review to the chart.

SQ3R

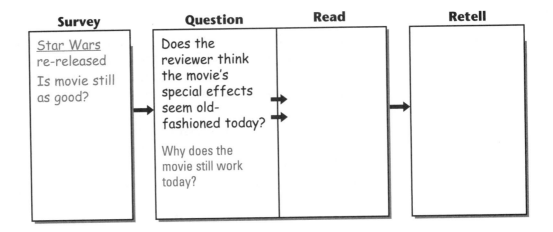

Survey	Question	Read	Retell
Star Wars re-released — Is movie still as good?	Does the reviewer think the movie's special effects seem old-fashioned today? Why does the movie still work today?		

Step 3. Read the selection.

Look for answers to your questions as you read. After you read, write your answers in the Read box. If you notice other important information, add it to the Read box, too. Be sure to include the main points in the review as well as any details that support them. The student answered her question in the SQ3R chart. Add answers to your questions and notes of your own about what you learned in the review.

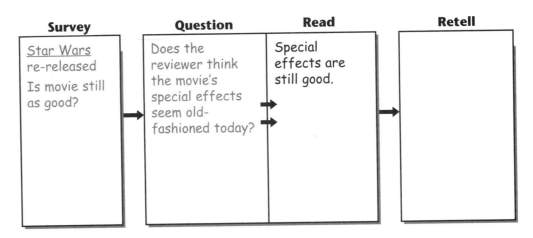

Survey	Question	Read	Retell
Star Wars re-released — Is movie still as good?	Does the reviewer think the movie's special effects seem old-fashioned today?	Special effects are still good.	

Star Wars Revisited

Star Wars landed on the scene like a galactic warship in 1977. No one had ever seen anything like it. Film distributors showed it reluctantly. It was a kiddie fantasy, they grumbled. Then the film opened—to rave reviews, large audiences, and even larger profits.

The Same Punch?
George Lucas decided to re-release the movie in 1997, 20 years later. Moviegoers wondered whether the movie would be as exciting

C3PO and R2-D2 from the movie *Star Wars*

the second time around. After all, they said, look what has happened to space movies in the last 20 years. *Star Wars*, of course, started that trend.

Today's movies have more breathtaking special effects and more graphic violence. It is harder to get moviegoers to say, "Wow." How would today's audience respond to the almost bloodless *Star Wars*? Would the movie seem too corny or too sweet to audiences that were used to the space movies of today?

The distributors also counted on viewers who had seen the original movie when they were children or teenagers. Would a movie that had been so important for so many people in their youth have the same impact years later? When people saw *Star Wars* the first time, many fell in love with the characters. They saw them as friends. Would people seeing the movie at a very different time in their lives be able to relive the emotions they had felt?

The distributors need not have feared. *Star Wars* is still a wonderful movie. If you haven't seen it, go. Even after two decades, the movie is still a wild ride. Even though special effects have been improved dramatically, the movie can still make a viewer gasp. The scene in which Luke Skywalker **maneuvers** his craft in and around the narrow walls of the Death Star still thrills. The famous club scene, with its hubbub of aliens, still makes a moviegoer laugh. No movie scene of alien–human interaction has anywhere near the power of that funny, yet oddly realistic scene.

Mythical Force

The story makes the movie work. When George Lucas wrote the script, he borrowed from almost every myth known to humankind. But yes, these myths still work. Luke still saves the princess. The forces of good still overcome the forces of evil. The cowboy-type guy with the heart of gold (Han Solo) still moves us. The soaring music still sends the message that good, decent people can overcome the forces of evil. It's a refreshing change from today's less positive movies.

"But I have it at home." I know that argument. Why should I spend money to see *Star Wars* when I can watch it at any time on video? If you've only seen the movie at home, you haven't had the experience. You haven't had the big-screen thrill, the life-sized airships swooping through the galaxy. You haven't heard the gasps and the laughs of your fellow moviegoers. *Star Wars* is fine at home. In a theater, though, it's much more. So pick yourself up off the couch and go to the movies. *Star Wars* provides a trip through the galaxy you'll never forget.

Vocabulary Tip

Look at clues in the sentence to figure out what *maneuvers* means. What does Luke do with his spacecraft?

READING STRATEGIES SQ3R

SQ3R

Step 4. Retell what you have learned.

When you retell what you have learned, you summarize it by putting the information into your own words. Putting an explanation into your own words means you have to think about all of the main points and choose the most important details.

Your next step is to write a summary of what you have learned from the movie review. Here is the beginning of the student's summary of the *Star Wars* review. Complete her summary of the review. You can use the notes you wrote in your SQ3R chart to help you.

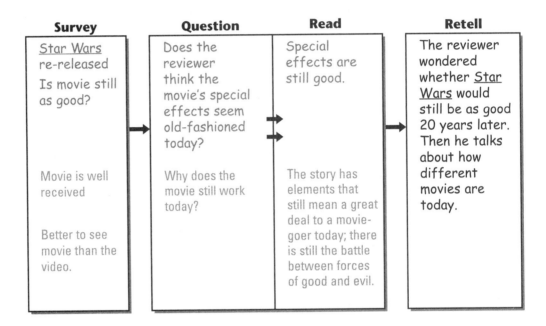

Survey	Question	Read	Retell
Star Wars re-released Is movie still as good? Movie is well received Better to see movie than the video.	Does the reviewer think the movie's special effects seem old-fashioned today? Why does the movie still work today?	Special effects are still good. The story has elements that still mean a great deal to a movie-goer today; there is still the battle between forces of good and evil.	The reviewer wondered whether Star Wars would still be as good 20 years later. Then he talks about how different movies are today.

Strategy Tip

Many people find that oral reviews help them make their main points more clearly.

Step 5. Review what you have learned.

Your last step is to review what you have learned. There are several ways you can review. You might go back to the questions you wrote in the Question box and see if you can answer them. You might discuss the review with a friend who has also read it. You might also check your memory by making a few notes about the review's main points. If you're unsure of a few details, survey the review again to find the sections that might have the information you need.

Apply It........... Now try the SQ3R strategy on a reading assignment you have. First, survey the selection. Then ask yourself questions about it. Next, read the selection. After you read, answer your questions and add notes that show the selection's main points. Then retell what you have learned by summarizing it. Finally, review what you have learned to check your understanding of your reading.

Lesson 5

U.S. History:
When the Rains Wouldn't Come

Understand It...... This selection is about something you might have heard of—the Dust Bowl. SQ3R is a good strategy for organizing information you already know and for organizing new information. Look at the headings and the photograph for hints about what you will learn in this selection.

Try It............... Think about the words *Dust Bowl*. You probably know something about that time in U.S. history. Below is a drawing of an SQ3R chart. Draw your own chart on a separate sheet of paper. Start your chart by doing a quick preview or survey of the article. Use what you learn to help you complete the survey column of the chart. Write some questions about what you might read. Then read the article and gather information to complete the entire chart.

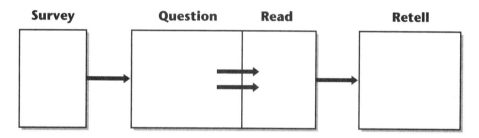

When the Rains Wouldn't Come

June 7, 1934 Sometimes it feels like we eat and drink dust. It's never far from our thoughts. Ma said today that she doesn't need a broom— she needs a shovel. She sounded really mad, but then Pa came in from the fields, and she put her head on his shoulder and cried.

June 21, 1934 Every day it looks like it's going to rain. The rain clouds join overhead, and they look like water, all heavy and black. But then, by late afternoon, they're gone and we're left again without rain. I saw Pa looking at the sky, and his shoulders slumped. Then he tried to cheer me up—"Don't worry, Scout, it'll rain." For some reason, that made me feel worse. His voice just didn't sound real. We both know if nothing changes, we'll have to leave.

June 22, 1934 I heard Ma and Pa talking. She was saying, "If we just hang on long enough, it'll change, John. It has to. Is all our work for nothing?" He just shook his head and shrugged his shoulders and then sat in the chair. "If it doesn't change soon, Margaret, we'll have no choice."

U.S. History: When the Rains Wouldn't Come

July 30, 1934 How can it possibly be—how can it go so long without rain? The dust blows into huge drifts that look almost like snow. People are leaving. I saw the Campbells go yesterday, everything packed up in their car. They sold out a couple of weeks ago, got just about nothing for all their stuff, Ma said. She said, under her breath, that it was giving up—but who could blame them? I wonder if we'll be leaving, too.

August 14, 1934 Ma and Pa have been talking to each other in low voices for about five days now. When I come into the room, they stop. I know we're leaving.

August 15, 1934 Sure enough, when I came down for breakfast, Ma and Pa sat Jordy and me down and told us, in these too-cheery voices, that we'll be starting a new life in California. They pulled out magazine pictures they had of the orange trees and the ocean, and they told us that's where we'll be going. Jordy said, in his anxious voice, "Can Peanut go?" Pa stopped a moment and then said, really gently, "Jordy, we won't have any room for a dog." So Jordy stormed out, crying his eyes out.

Strategy Tip

What does the photograph show you about the Dust Bowl? Ask questions that you can add to the Question column on your SQ3R chart.

Look at the people. Look at the house. What do they tell you about the amount of dust there is?

August 19, 1934 It didn't take long, once they had made up their minds. It's nothing to them, I guess, to leave a place we've lived our whole lives. They don't care. We sold everything—the one cow we had left, the farm equipment. Nobody wanted most of the stuff in our house, so we left it. It was strange, just seeing those things sitting there, like they are waiting for us to come back. Jordy's not speaking to Ma and Pa because Peanut isn't going. Pa is out there now, finishing the packing. Ma couldn't bear to part with her good dishes, so Pa **strapped** them on the top of the car in a special box. We're leaving first thing tomorrow.

August 20, 1934 I looked back at the house and the farm as long as I could. Maybe Oklahoma wasn't the best place ever, but it is home. It was strange, leaving. Nobody came to see us off. Most of our friends are gone already. The ones that are left seem too beaten down to do much

Vocabulary Tip

If you know that a *strap* is a "piece of flexible material used to hold something down," you can figure out that the verb *strapped* means "to hold something with a strap."

of anything. Maybe it will be wonderful in California, with the ocean and the orange trees. I keep that thought in my mind.

August 25, 1934 We don't have much money, so we camp along the way and buy a little food at a time. I hear Ma and Pa talking about money all the time. They're afraid we won't have enough money to get us to California.

August 31, 1934 All along the way we've been seeing people who look just like us. They have everything they own on their cars or in their trucks. They're all headed for California. How could there be enough work for everybody? I also found out that all of us travelers have a bad name. People call us "Okies" because we're from Oklahoma. The way they say it, though—they spit it out like it's a bad word and we're bad people. I saw Ma flinch when we went to a service station to ask for water and the man there swore at her and called her an Okie.

September 1, 1934 We've been playing a game—what will life be like in California? Ma imagines the smell of flowers and fruit everywhere and the breeze from the ocean. I think of rain and green and a big white house with a grass yard. Pa talks about working and saving enough to buy a farm there, a farm where tomatoes grow as big as his fist. Jordy talks about going back home and getting Peanut so he can live with us.

September 3, 1934 We're in California. It's not so great. There are people just like us everywhere, camped in ugly yards of dirt. When Pa asks where to go to get work, they look at him like he's crazy. "Don't you think we'd have work if we knew?" one man said to him, glaring. Now I'm scared. What if there isn't any work here, either? What will we do? How will we live?

After you finish reading, review what you have learned by writing a summary of the selection. Use your SQ3R chart to help you.

Apply It. . . . . To check your understanding of the diary entries, circle the best answer to each of the following questions.

1. Which of the following is *incorrect*?
   a. The family swore never to leave Oklahoma.
   b. Every day it looks like rain, but the rain doesn't come.
   c. People use the word *Okie* as an insult.
   d. The family travels from Oklahoma to California.

Test Tip

Look closely at the wording of questions. The word *incorrect* in question 1 tells you that three of the answers are correct, or true, according to the diary.

U.S. History:
When the Rains Wouldn't Come

2. You could describe the narrator as
   a. a worried child.
   b. a lonely child.
   c. a family pet.
   d. an unhappy parent.

3. In the August 31 entry, the word *flinch* means
   a. to spit.
   b. to say a swear word.
   c. to make a quick movement backward.
   d. to insult someone.

4. The travelers from Oklahoma probably have a bad reputation because
   a. they are considered bad luck.
   b. there are many of them and they are poor.
   c. they are lazy.
   d. they make traffic on the roads.

5. The diary writer's mood when the family first decides to leave could best be described as
   a. happy.
   b. accepting.
   c. furious.
   d. unconcerned.

Use the lines below to write your answers for numbers 6 and 7. Use your SQ3R chart to help you.

6. Write a summary of the important events that occur in these entries.

The diary begins with the rain not coming and how the farm family may have to leave their home. The parents decide to leave, pack the family's belongings on the car, and leave for California. When they arrive, they begin to look for work.

7. Imagine that you are the diary writer. Do you think you would feel the same? Would you feel differently? Explain your answer.

Sample answer: I would feel more sad than the diary writer does, because it would be very hard to leave a place where I had spent my life and very hard to leave my dog.

Lesson 6

Civics:
The Celebration Experiment

Understand It...... Almost everyone has had some contact with the Walt Disney Company. Many people have seen Disney movies. Others have been to a Disney theme park. Disney is part of America. Try using the SQ3R strategy to help you understand the selection. It will help you focus your thoughts before you read. It will also help you read actively.

Try It.............. Draw an SQ3R chart like the one below on a separate sheet of paper. First, preview the article. Write what you think you will read in the Survey column. Use key words or phrases you found while previewing. Then write questions about the article in the Question column. Read the article. After you read, fill in the Read column. You should be able to answer your questions in this column. Complete your chart by retelling what you have learned in the Retell column. Finally, Review what you have learned.

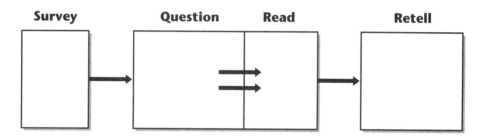

The Celebration Experiment

What happens when Mickey Mouse meets politics? The answer is Celebration, Florida. This new city was built by Disney. Every detail has been planned, even the color of the curtains people may hang in their windows. Everything is perfect. Or is it? Can a company run a town? That is the question Celebration hopes to answer.

Part of the answer, of course, has to do with the company. Almost everyone in the United States probably has an opinion about Disney. To some, *Disney* means clean, wholesome entertainment. It means warm feelings. It means organization. It means that every detail is in place. To others, *Disney* means too much organization. It means forced happiness. It means nothing above average. It means boring.

You can probably guess how the two groups feel about Celebration. The pro-Disney group is lining up to get in. The anti-Disney group is warning of grim results. The interesting question, though, is whether a company used to managing theme parks will be able to manage a town. In Celebration, Disney can't fire anyone. The company can't force people to do what they don't want to do.

Civics:
The Celebration Experiment

The Disney Dream

Celebration is not a new idea. The form it took is new. For years, Walt Disney dreamed of building a city of the future. In Disney's mind, that city would be built under a dome. It would have skyscrapers. Residents would travel by monorail. No retirees would be allowed. Nobody would own property. Instead, the city would be home to young renters. Before that town was built, however, Walt Disney died.

The city that has risen from the ground in Florida is very different from Walt Disney's dream city. Celebration is intended to remind people of a simpler time. Disney is trying to sell the city as a return to a simpler time. The dream is that this would be a place where neighbors sit on their front porches and talk to one another. In this new community, crime would be low and neighbors would be friendly.

To create that **utopia**, a place where life is perfect, Disney put some very good minds to work. The company hired some of the best designers in the business. It hired nationally known architects. What some of those people are doing in Celebration is a dream for them, too. Many architects have long argued that suburbs are not the best places to live. They say that suburbs isolate people. People drive into their garages, go into their houses, and never come out.

Celebration was designed with older **principles** in mind. Houses have front porches. Streets are designed so neighbors can meet. That is what people like, the planners say. Their aim is to keep the best of the old ways of designing cities. There is a name for this design theory: New Urbanism.

The New Reality

Disney's town attracted attention from the moment it was announced. For some people, just knowing Disney was involved made the project look great. Others liked the idea of creating an old-time town. Still others looked at the state-of-the-art school and decided to buy in Celebration.

Disney's town, Celebration

Many people joined a lottery to buy housing there. That there was a lottery at all is noteworthy. People wanted to live in this town. There will eventually be 8,000 homes there. The population will be 15,000 to 20,000. Housing isn't cheap, either. A house here costs more than in the areas around Celebration.

Vocabulary Tip

Notice that the definition for *utopia*, "a place where life is perfect," appears between commas right after the word.

Vocabulary Tip

The word *principle* has a homophone, *principal*. These words are spelled differently and have different meanings, but they sound the same. You can tell which one is correct by reading the sentence and deciding which meaning makes more sense.

Most of the people who first came out to see the new town were upper- or middle-class whites. Although Disney plans to provide places for people who have less money, there is no housing for poor people.

One of the unusual aspects of the town is that there will be no city government. The county will take care of water and sewers. Disney will take care of everything else. The company promises to listen to the homeowners' group. That group will pass judgment on people who break rules. Those rules include what color homes can be painted. One woman decided not to fight, and she took her red curtains down. Another couple fought for their right to have a front door that is different from the plans—and won.

Some of the residents think the idea of Disney control is great. They think Disney will make the right decisions. They trust Disney more than any politicians, they say. On the other hand, real life is messy. Things happen in a real town that don't happen in a theme park.

People who follow local politics are watching the growth of Celebration with great interest. Can Disney make it work? Can it really replace government? Can Disney govern better than politicians? The future of this Florida town has a lot to teach anyone who is interested in democracy in America.

Now review your SQ3R chart. Did you find answers to all your questions? If you didn't, you may want to look back at the article. You can also find articles about Disney and Celebration in magazines and on the Internet. Then use your SQ3R chart to write a summary of the article. Use the summary and your SQ3R chart to help you answer the following questions.

Apply It. . . . . To check your understanding of the article, circle the best answer to each of the following questions.

Test Tip

Question 2 asks for the main idea of the article. When a question asks for the main idea, more than one answer may have correct information, but only one answer is the *main idea* of the article.

1. Walt Disney's ideas for a town included
   a. front porches on every house.
   b. skyscrapers and a monorail.
   c. a population with many different ages of people.
   d. home ownership for everyone.

2. The main idea of this article is that
   a. Celebration has attracted attention from around the country.
   b. the Disney company has created another brilliant idea.
   c. Celebration is an experiment to see if a company can run a town.
   d. Celebration will make huge profits for Disney.

Civics:
The Celebration Experiment

3. The phrase *New Urbanism* in the section "The Disney Dream" means
   a. keeping the best of the old ways of designing cities.
   b. mixing old and new design ideas.
   c. finding new ways of designing cities.
   d. making sure that everyone in a city can get onto the highway.

4. People who said they were interested in living in Celebration
   a. were often interested because of the Disney name.
   b. wanted to buy in an affordable area.
   c. usually didn't know Disney had created the town.
   d. wanted to move there because the town would be modern.

5. The author believes that the most interesting question about Celebration is whether
   a. Disney can make a profit.
   b. a big corporation can successfully replace government.
   c. people will be happy living in a town run by a company.
   d. the New Urbanism will work.

Use the lines below to write your answers for numbers 6 and 7. You can use your SQ3R chart to help you.

6. What are the major arguments for and against Celebration? Summarize them here.

The arguments for Celebration are that Disney is spending time and money trying to design a town that people will love and that the Disney name is a guarantee that the town will be run well. The arguments against Celebration are that Disney is too organized, that the town will be boring, and that Disney is too controlling.

7. Why do you think the idea of Celebration changed so much from Walt Disney's original dream? Support your ideas.

Sample answer: Ideas changed from the time Walt Disney first created the idea of Celebration. In addition, the designers and architects believed in New Urbanism; their aim was to keep the best of the old ways of designing cities.

Lesson 7

Geography: The Race for Longitude

Understand It...... This selection discusses a problem that people tried to solve for centuries: how to calculate longitude. You may not know much about how to find longitude. Because the SQ3R strategy relies on surveying before you read, it can help you get the most from this selection.

Try It............. On another sheet of paper, draw an SQ3R like the one shown below. Then survey, or preview, the selection, looking at the title, the subheadings, the topic sentences, and the map. What questions do they suggest to you?

In the Survey box, write key words or phrases you found while surveying. Then write your questions in the Question box. After you read, write the answers to your questions in the Read box. Then summarize the selection in the Retell box. You will then review what you have read to check your understanding.

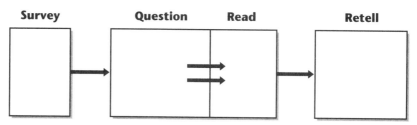

Strategy Tip

When you survey, let your eyes pass quickly over the selection. Look for key words and phrases that can tell you what the selection is about.

Vocabulary Tip

The terms *latitude* and *longitude* are introduced here. In many texts, boldfaced terms often are followed by definitions.

The Race for Longitude

When you look at a globe, you see the imaginary lines of **latitude** and **longitude**. These lines help people figure out exactly where they are on Earth. Latitude shows distance north or south of the equator. The equator is a line of latitude that circles the globe and divides it into the Northern Hemisphere and the Southern Hemisphere. Longitude is the distance east or west of a given point.

Today, we have maps to guide us that use these lines. However, lines of latitude and longitude did not always exist.

An Old Problem

The idea of longitude and latitude is at least as old as 300 B.C. The Greek scientist Ptolemy, who lived in the second century, plotted longitude and latitude on maps.

For centuries, sailors had known how to determine latitude. A sailor used a sextant, an instrument that measures the altitude of the sun as it passes overhead. Then the sailor looked at a book that told about the movement of the sun and stars. By putting the information together, a sailor could determine the ship's latitude.

Longitude was trickier because it can't be measured using the stars and the sun. Many people had already tried to solve the longitude problem.

Geography:
The Race for Longitude

Strategy Tip

Use the map to review your understanding of latitude and longitude. How might not knowing a ship's exact location cause trouble?

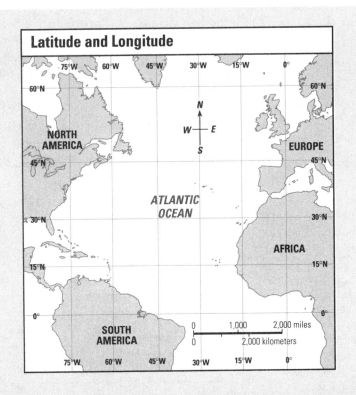

Latitude and Longitude

For ocean travel, the problem was critical. If a sea captain couldn't determine his ship's exact location, he could miss his destination by hundreds of miles. In addition, many ships were wrecked because they didn't know exactly where they were.

A Prize for Longitude

In 1714, the British Parliament decided the problem had become a crisis. Parliament offered a huge reward to the person who could find a way to calculate longitude. Today, that prize would be worth about $12 million.

Some seekers of the prize decided to navigate using astronomy. They thought that by measuring the distance between the moon and certain stars, then comparing that measurement to known positions at home, they could calculate longitude. Most people took this approach.

Others thought that the way to solve the problem involved creating a timepiece that could keep perfect time on the ocean. As early as 1530, a Flemish astronomer had thought this might be the key. In 1727, an English clockmaker named John Harrison chose to try to solve the longitude problem in this way.

If a sailor knew the exact time both at sea and at another location— at the same moment—he could pinpoint how far east or west the ship was.

Strategy Tip

Think about each subheading as you survey. What does each one tell you about the topic? Add these thoughts to your SQ3R chart.

Sailors could determine their location in this way because Earth makes one full revolution, or 360 degrees, per day. Each hour equals one 24th of a revolution, or 15 degrees. That means that if there is an hour's difference between noon at sea and the time at home, the ship has traveled 15 degrees longitude to the east or west. It seems clear, then, that time is the best way to determine longitude. However, this solution presented a problem.

In the 18th century, clocks that stood in one place were mostly reliable. No clock, though, could keep time accurately if it moved from one place to another. Keeping time on a ship presented even more difficulties. Pendulums swung with the waves. Clock oil became thicker or thinner when a ship sailed from a cold place to a warm place. Metal parts contracted or expanded with temperature changes. A slight difference in temperature could mean a completely wrong calculation for a ship's **navigator**.

An Unlikely Prizewinner

John Harrison was not a famous scientist. He had begun his working life as a carpenter. He had later started making clocks. His lack of formal training made his accomplishment even more remarkable.

Harrison created a new kind of clock. There was almost no friction between the parts, which meant they would not stick and become unreliable. The parts did not need to be oiled or cleaned. The parts also stayed in place, no matter how much a ship rolled.

In 1735, Harrison sent the first of his clocks to the British Board of Longitude. Like most of the scientists of the day, the board's members thought that the moon-and-stars solution was the best choice. They were less interested in an idea that relied on something as simple as a clock.

Harrison's clocks worked. Sailors praised them. However, Reverend Nevil Maskelyne, who was himself searching for a way to determine longitude by using the moon and stars, became an enemy of Harrison's.

Maskelyne sat on the board that would decide the prize. He used some unfair **tactics** to keep the prize from Harrison, such as changing the rules of the contest. Finally, when enough sailors showed that Harrison's method worked, the clockmaker attracted the notice of King George III. In 1773, Harrison received the prize. Three years later, he died.

Today, Harrison's shipboard clocks are part of history. For many decades, Harrison's invention made the difference between life and death for sailors around the world.

Vocabulary Tip

When you see *-or* or *-er* at the end of a noun, it may mean "one who does." For example, the word *navigator* means "one who navigates."

Vocabulary Tip

You can figure out the meaning of *tactics* by reading the sentence carefully. An example is given of Maskelyne's tactics: changing the rules of the contest. So *tactics* are "ways to achieve a goal."

Look over your SQ3R notes. Do they show the selection's main points? Add notes on these points to the Read box. In the Retell box, review the selection by writing a summary. Then review what you learned by comparing answers to the questions on the next page with a classmate.

Geography:
The Race for Longitude

To check your understanding of the selection, circle the best answer to each question below.

Test Tip

Notice that the choices for question 1 have two parts. Both parts must be correct for an answer to be correct.

1. The difference between longitude and latitude is that
   a. longitude lines run east to west and latitude lines run south to north.
   b. longitude lines run north to south and latitude lines run east to west.
   c. longitude lines are north of the equator and latitude lines are south of the equator.
   d. longitude lines are south of the equator and latitude lines are north of the equator.

2. Finding a way to determine longitude was important because
   a. it was easier to fight wars when ships could find one another.
   b. ships could not travel safely without it.
   c. ships needed more accurate clocks.
   d. sailors already knew how to determine latitude.

3. In the fourth paragraph in the section "A Prize for Longitude," *pinpoint* means
   a. sharpen.
   b. locate approximately.
   c. locate exactly.
   d. work well.

4. You might infer that the British Board of Longitude supported the idea of using astronomy to determine longitude because
   a. the board wanted to make sure no one won the prize.
   b. Harrison's clocks kept failing.
   c. King George III preferred the astronomy idea.
   d. it seemed more logical to them than the clock solution.

5. What do you think happened as a result of Harrison's solution?
   a. More people were able to travel on long sea voyages.
   b. Long sea voyages became safer.
   c. People kept trying to prove Harrison wrong.
   d. Fewer ships went on long sea voyages.

Use the lines below to write your answers for numbers 6 and 7. Use your SQ3R notes to help you.

6. Why was longitude so much more difficult to determine than latitude?

Sailors could determine latitude by using a sextant to measure the altitude of the sun and knowing the movements of the sun and stars. Calculating longitude meant knowing not only the time where the ship was, but also the time at another place. For centuries, clocks were not accurate enough to depend on.

7. Why could Harrison's clock work to determine longitude when other clocks could not?

Harrison's clock succeeded because there was almost no friction between the parts, it needed no oiling, it didn't need to be cleaned, and the parts stayed in place regardless of the ship's movement.

Lesson 8

Civics:
A Debate on Slavery

Understand It...... This selection consists of two writers' views on enslavement during the years before the Civil War. You probably already know something about enslavement, which many people view as a shameful part of U.S. history. Because some questions probably come to mind as soon as you read the title, SQ3R is a good strategy to use with this debate.

Try It............. Copy the SQ3R chart below onto another sheet of paper. Before you begin reading, survey, or preview, the article to get an idea of the authors' arguments. In the Survey box, write key words or phrases you found.

Then write some questions you have about the debate in the Question box. After you read, take notes in the Read box. Be sure to look for answers to the questions you asked. When you have finished reading and creating your chart, you will write a summary of the debate in the Retell box. Finally, you will review what you have learned by listing the debaters' opinions.

Strategy Tip

You know from previewing that each author wants to persuade readers that his argument is correct. As you read, make sure you note each major argument or example the authors use.

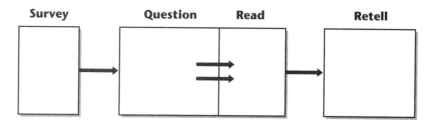

A Debate on Slavery
Taken from two editorials that appeared in
The Margins, a national newspaper, in 1850

Slavery Is a Force for Good, by Peter Owens

As a Southerner, I know slavery well. I am grateful to the owners of this newspaper for the chance to explain what every Southerner knows: Slavery is not an evil, but a force for good.

There are many who disagree, I know. They have no idea what pain their good intentions would cause, not just to slave-owners but also to the slaves themselves.

As a slaveholder, I have the well-being of around 200 human souls, Africans, as a burden I carry daily. These people are not what the readers of this paper would consider citizens. Instead, they are more like children. They are certainly capable of doing the work I give them to do. I have seen no evidence that any of my slaves, if set free, would be able to function outside the shelter of my plantation.

You have to know more of the history of these people. They come from a land where slavery is common. They understand the system well. Many were probably slaves in Africa. If they were not slaves, their parents might have been. They understand and have done well under the system.

Civics:
A Debate on Slavery

In contrast to the lives they would lead on their home continent, my slaves have enough to eat. They have shelter and clothing. They have the comfort of their friends. I would be a fool not to treat them well. If I were to mistreat them, they would be less able to work. Besides that, they are in my care. It is my duty to treat them well, a charge I took on when I bought them, a charge I take very seriously.

Let us think of the fate of my slaves if I were to grant them their freedom. Most would feel I was punishing them. They would not know where to go or what to do. They would be helpless in life's harsh tide.

In many ways, I envy my slaves. None of us is really free. We all have our masters, our bosses, the men to whom we owe money, the God to whom we owe respect. My slaves, however, know the limits of their lives. They are happy and productive within those limits. They have everything they need. In the South today, slavery works.

I have asked you to imagine the fate of my slaves if I were to abandon them. Imagine, now, the fate of my plantation and the rest of the South. This is a strong economy, but it is not like the economy of the North. Our economy is based on slavery. Without it, the South crumbles and perhaps the nation as well. Can you dispose of slavery, knowing it may well lead to a nation's ruin? In this situation, I argue, even if my other claims were all false, freeing the slaves would mean a national crisis. Can we allow that?

I believe it is much better to leave the situation as it is. As I say, my slaves are happy and healthy. They understand their place. Destroying this entire way of life to satisfy a few Northern **do-gooders** who have no knowledge of what they are destroying would profit no one.

Slavery Is Nothing But Evil, by Nixon Barnes

I do not need long, twisted arguments about the economy and the happiness of men in chains. My beliefs are based on a simple statement: It is wrong for one human being to own another.

Our founding fathers were correct: All men are created equal, whether they are slaves or kings. Equality means, of course, that slavery is wrong. I'd like to illustrate this idea with the story of a typical slave.

His life begins in Africa, in a village where generations of his family have grown up. He is a loving father, a loving husband, a man who has his family with him. He is a good worker. He makes sure his family has enough food, sturdy shelter, and warm clothing.

Then, one terrible day, raiders burst into this man's village, kidnapping him and many other healthy young adults. He is dragged in chains to a coastal city, where he is sold to a man who makes his living buying human flesh. And what will happen to his family?

Vocabulary Tip

You can understand the term *do-gooders* by putting together the parts of the word. Also look at the way the word is used in the sentence.

From there, he endures a terrible voyage on the ocean. Many of those on the ship die and are dumped overboard. Many others are constantly sick. All the slaves are kept in the hold of the ship. They are chained together. They see the sun only rarely.

Once on the shores of this country, he is displayed on a stage, like a horse, and sold. From there he is chained again and taken to a plantation in the South. There, alone, thousands of miles from his wife and children, he is forced to work from sunup to sundown. He has only enough food to keep him alive, because food is expensive. He has only enough clothing to cover himself. His living quarters are a disgrace. When he protests, he is beaten—you can see the deep marks of the lash, which cover his back. This is his fate until the day he dies. Can anyone not believe that a great wrong is occurring?

Strategy Tip

How does this illustration support Barnes's arguments?

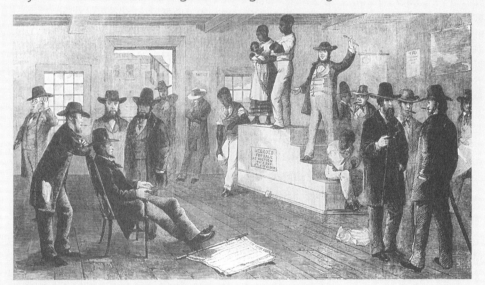

A Virginia slave auction from *London Illustrated News*, Feb. 16, 1861

Can anyone not hear these facts without feeling deep shame that our country permits this outrageous sin to exist? If we are to remain a people with even a hint of virtue, we must end slavery.

Slaveholders will tell you that their slaves are better off. Who are they to decide what is better for another human being? Africans are people as much as any Southern planter and, in many respects, much better ones. They have not stripped others of their humanity, their dignity, their freedom. If anything, the slaves are the ones who should decide the fate of their masters.

Slavery is morally wrong. Until it is banned, we can never raise our heads high with pride. A country that permits the slavery of a human being is not a country that deserves God's blessing or men's praise.

Civics:
A Debate on Slavery

After you finish reading, complete your SQ3R notes. Then write a summary of each author's argument in the Retell box. Finally, review what you learned by listing the debaters' opinions from memory.

Apply It. . . . . To check your understanding of the debate, circle the best answer to each question below.

1. Which of the following is *not* an argument that Peter Owens uses?
   a. The enslaved people are happier in the United States than in Africa.
   b. It is God's will that Africans should be enslaved.
   c. The South might crumble if slavery ended.
   d. For Africans, enslavement is better than freedom.

Test Tip

Question 2 asks you what Owens *infers* in his argument. This means that he did not state the answer to this question directly. Think about what Owens said. Then decide which choice sounds like an argument Owens would make.

2. Peter Owens infers that he and his slaves are similar because
   a. they can make their own decisions.
   b. every person has a boss or master.
   c. all people know what is good for them.
   d. both a and b

3. One fact that Barnes and Owens disagree about is
   a. how well enslaved people are treated on plantations.
   b. how important the slave trade is to the South.
   c. how much enslaved people add to the economy.
   d. how most enslaved people came to this country.

4. In the fifth paragraph of Barnes's editorial, the word *endures* means
   a. enjoys.
   b. lives through.
   c. forgets.
   d. remembers.

Test Tip

Question 5 asks for the *most important* reason Barnes told this story. More than one answer might be correct, but only one answer is the *most important*.

5. The *most important* reason for Barnes to tell about the slave ships is that
   a. he thought the story showed what the voyage to America was like.
   b. no one thought about how enslaved people got to the United States.
   c. he wanted to show how terrible slave buyers were.
   d. he did not want people to debate the issue of enslavement.

Use the lines below to write your answers for numbers 6 and 7. Use your SQ3R chart to help you.

6. Contrast Owens's and Barnes's descriptions of enslaved people.

According to Owens, the slaves are happy, childlike, and unable to live on their own. They are well-fed, -housed, and -clothed, and are not mistreated. Barnes says the slaves are miserable; long for freedom; are ill-housed, -clothed, and -fed; and are treated poorly.

7. Choose one of the arguments and write a response to it. You may use arguments the opposing author used.

Sample answer: Slaves are not children. They are people who should have rights, including the right to freedom. The slaves were not necessarily slaves in Africa. There is plenty of evidence that slaves are mistreated. You have only to look at the backs of some slaves and see the whip marks to know that. If the South's economy fails, so be it. People must find a way of surviving that does not depend on the blood of others. Slavery is immoral.

Unit 2 Review: SQ3R

In this unit, you have practiced using the SQ3R reading strategy. Use this strategy when you read the selection below. Use a separate sheet of paper to draw a chart, take notes, and summarize what you learn.

Hint *Remember that all reading strategies have activities for before, during, and after reading. To review these steps, look at the inside back cover of this book.*

The Legend of the Pony Express

A Pony Express rider gallops across the plains, delivering the news that Abraham Lincoln has been elected President of the United States. That image of the Pony Express rider is one of the most exciting of the West. It has become part of the legend of the frontier.

The Pony Express began on April 3, 1860. The company boasted that its riders would deliver the mail from St. Joseph, Missouri, to Sacramento, California, in eight to ten days. Although the postage was extremely expensive at first, that was half the time it took by stagecoach.

Making the 2,000-mile trip in that time seemed impossible. The trip from Missouri to California was a race against time. Each rider was expected to travel 75 miles a day. During a day, the rider would change horses at stations about ten miles apart.

When the first mail pouch arrived in California ten days after leaving Missouri, its rider galloped into Sacramento's streets and brass bands played. Suddenly, the West Coast seemed linked with the East.

Special saddlebags had been designed for the Pony Express. They could easily be moved from horse to horse as the mail moved across the country. As a rider arrived at a station, he had two minutes to grab the square leather saddlebag. Attached to the bag were four leather boxes with the mail. The rider threw the saddlebag over the next horse's back and was off.

The riders were young men, usually teenagers. They were not only expert riders but they were also lightweight. They were known for their bravery as well as for their ability. In the time the service operated, only one mail delivery was lost. Rider Buffalo Bill Cody, who was 15 when he rode for the Pony Express, once spent 21 hours in the saddle, covering 320 miles. The riders who were to replace him had failed to appear.

As the first Pony Express rider took off, telegraph lines had begun

Unit 2 Review: SQ3R

to creep from East to West. On October 22, 1861, the lines met in Salt Lake City. Two days later, the Pony Express ended.

Despite its exciting history, the Pony Express lasted only 18 months. The company's expenses were enormous. It had 200 riders, and about 500 ponies stabled at 150 locations along the route. Its owners lost $200,000 and declared bankruptcy. Even so, for many, the Pony Express is the perfect example of the excitement of the Wild West.

Use your SQ3R chart to help you answer the questions below.

1. Why was the arrival of the first Pony Express rider greeted in Sacramento with such enthusiasm?
   a. Finally, there was an inexpensive way to send mail from coast to coast.
   b. Because the mail only took ten days from Missouri to California, the West Coast finally felt linked to the East.
   c. The owners of the company wanted the newspapers to report the arrival of the first Pony Express.
   d. both a and b

2. Which is the best description of Pony Express riders?
   a. men who knew the horses they were to ride extremely well
   b. expert riders who were large enough to control the horses
   c. teenagers who knew the land they were to ride very well
   d. teenagers hired for their light weight and ability

3. Why did the Pony Express end service?
   a. The company could not find enough reliable riders.
   b. The cost of the service was too high.
   c. Telegraph lines linked the East with the West.
   d. The company's owners became tired of losing money.

4. Describe a trip by the Pony Express from Missouri to California.

   During the 2,000 mile trip from Missouri to Sacramento, each rider would travel 75 miles a day.
   Riders would change horses about every ten miles and travel at top speed throughout their journey.

   _____

5. How do you think the country changed when the West Coast and East Coast were linked?

   Sample answer: People from both coasts could now share knowledge and ideas. This communication
   was a way to unify the country.

   _____

Unit 3 Strategy: **PLAN**

Understand It...... PLAN works well for people who learn best when they can make a picture of what they are learning. PLAN stands for **P**redict, **L**ocate, **A**dd, and **N**ote. When you use PLAN, you create a word map that predicts what you will read.

There are many ways to draw word maps. If all the information in a reading relates to one subject, you might draw a wheel with spokes.

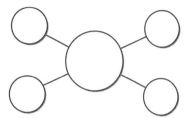

If an article compares and contrasts several different things, a Venn diagram might work best. Write the ideas the subjects have in common in the space that links both circles. Write the information that is true of only one subject in the outside of one circle.

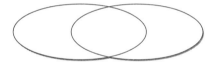

If an article is organized by time, you can create a sequence chart. In a sequence chart, you write events in the order in which they happen. Arrows connect the boxes.

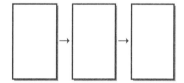

Maybe you know another way to show how a piece of writing is organized. Feel free to draw any kind of word map that helps you organize the information you're learning.

Try It............... Once you choose a graphic, you locate and add information to it that tells you whether your ideas were right. Then you fill in the map with that information. Finally, you note your understanding of what you read.

On pages 51–52 is an article about Koko, a gorilla who learned sign language. To help her understand the article, a student used PLAN as she read. Read along to see how to use PLAN.

PLAN

Step 1. Predict what you will learn.

When the student first looked at the article, she didn't see any subheadings. She previewed the paragraphs to see what the article was about. She noticed that the article did not compare two things. This told her that she couldn't use a Venn diagram.

Then she noticed that the article was not written in time order, so she decided not to use a sequence chart. Finally, she decided that everything in the article was about one subject—a gorilla named Koko—so she started a wheel-and-spoke diagram. She put Koko's name in the middle. Then she arranged around it information she knew about Koko.

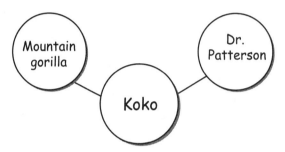

Now preview the selection and make your own predictions about what will be in the article. Use the diagram below to begin using the PLAN strategy. Write the topic—Koko—in the middle circle. Write the main points you think the article will contain in the connecting circles. Add circles as you need them to fit other points.

Strategy Tip
Leave enough space in your diagram so you can add more circles. These circles will contain other main points you find and information about each point.

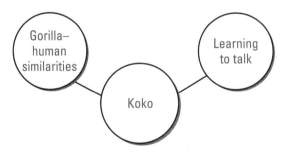

Step 2. Locate information you will look for as you read.

Look at your diagram. Put check marks next to ideas or people you know something about. Put a question mark next to anything unfamiliar to you. Marking your diagram will help you think about what you already know about the subject and will prepare you to understand what you will read. Here's what the student thought as she created her diagram:

I think I've heard of Koko, so I'll put a check mark there. I also know something about mountain gorillas, so I'll check that. I've never heard of Dr. Patterson, so I'll write a question mark by her name.

The student's wheel-and-spoke diagram now looked like this:

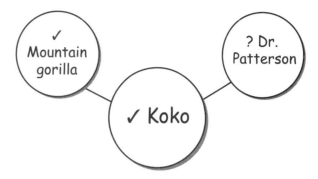

Locate ideas or people you know something about on your diagram. Place check marks there. Put question marks in front of ideas or people you know nothing about.

Step 3. Read, then add information to your map.

Read the selection about Koko. Then write words or short phrases that remind you of the supporting facts or details under each main point. If you missed major points, add them to the diagram, along with details that support them.

Here's how the student began filling in her diagram:

Strategy Tip

Don't copy the article on your diagram. Use key words or short phrases that remind you only of the main points.

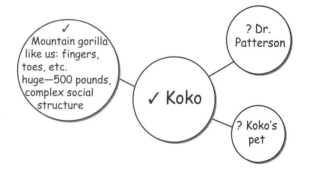

After you read, fill in your own diagram. Add major points and write words that will remind you of evidence or details for each point.

Vocabulary Tip

Even if you don't know the word *genetic,* you might have heard the word *gene.* Genes are the building blocks of cells that make us who we are. *Genetic* is a word that describes something related to genes.

Koko, the Talking Gorilla

We all know that animals can communicate. A cat's purr can tell us it loves being petted. Dogs mope when they have done something wrong. However, a gorilla is different. When a mountain gorilla named Koko began understanding human language and reacting to it, people took note.

Gorillas and humans belong to the same **genetic** family. Gorillas have arms and legs, as we do. They also have ten fingers and ten toes. They have

PLAN

Koko and Dr. Patterson

32 teeth. Their faces look a little like ours. They are much bigger than we are, though. A full-grown male can be taller than 6 feet and weigh about 500 pounds. In the wild, gorillas care for their young and play with one another. They have a complex social structure that's similar in many ways to ours.

In 1972, Dr. Penny Patterson was a graduate student at Stanford University. She saw Koko at the San Francisco Zoo, where she was doing a study. Koko had been sick, and she wasn't living with the other gorillas. The zoo officials were afraid she would die without special care.

At about that time, Patterson went to a talk about a chimpanzee that had learned 132 words in sign language. Patterson decided to find out whether a gorilla could learn sign language. She also wanted to help Koko. Within weeks, Patterson had taught Koko a few words in American Sign Language (ASL). People who use ASL make hand motions instead of saying words. Koko was the first gorilla to learn a human language.

Patterson began her study 25 years ago. Since then, Koko has learned 800 signs and 2,000 English words. One year, she told Patterson she wanted a cat for her birthday. Patterson gave her a toy cat. Koko responded by signing, "That red." To Koko, the word red means "angry." Koko didn't want a toy. She wanted a real cat.

Finally, she got one. Patterson's assistant brought three kittens to the lab. Koko played with one. She signed, "Cat do scratch. Koko love." Koko cared for the cat. She played with her. When the cat died after being hit by a car, Koko cried.

In 1976, Patterson began the Gorilla Foundation. The foundation helps save the habitat of the mountain gorilla. Today, about 600 mountain gorillas still live in the wild. The members also work to save other animals that live in the African rain forest.

Strategy Tip

Some readers find that using different-colored highlighters can help them remember what they read. They highlight the main points in one color and the supporting details in another color. This step can help you remember what you read.

Step 4. Note what you have learned.

Now review your diagram. If it does not show how the article is organized, you may want to redo it. Close your eyes and review the important points or write a summary. Then redraw your diagram. In addition to checking your understanding of your reading, you can use your diagram as a study guide. The notes you made will help you review for tests.

Apply It. . . . .

Strategy Tip

Try different strategies to help you remember what you read. Use the method that works best for you.

Use the PLAN strategy with a reading assignment you have. Preview the reading, looking for the way the information is organized. If there is one main topic, make a wheel-and-spoke diagram. If your assignment compares two people or ideas, use a Venn diagram. If the assignment tells events in time order, try a sequence chart. Then read and revise your drawing if necessary. As a last step, make notes about what you've learned to help you remember the main points of the reading.

Lesson 9

U.S. History: The Underground Railroad

Understand It...... The PLAN strategy should help you understand this selection because you can choose the graphic that makes sense to you. First, preview this selection. If it's written in chronological, or time, order, use the sequence chart. If it compares and contrasts two things, use the Venn diagram. If it focuses on one topic, a wheel-and-spoke diagram could be your best choice. Once you decide how the selection is organized, choose the graphic you think best fits it.

Try It.............. Remember that when you use the PLAN strategy, you preview to find out more about what you'll be reading. You use that information to predict what the main points may be. You use the information about the main points to sketch your graphic. Then you read again, locating important information. You put check marks next to information you know something about and question marks next to information you know little about. Finally, you add information that supports the main points. If you missed main points, add them, too.

Below you'll find three possible PLAN graphics. You can use one of them or create a graphic of your own.

Strategy Tip
If you put a question mark in front of a point, make sure you understand it by the time you finish reading.

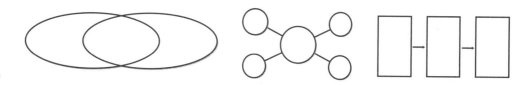

Vocabulary Tip
You might not know what *bounty hunters* are. However, you know what *hunters* are. Who might chase enslaved people? Those who returned enslaved people could claim a *bounty*, or reward.

The Underground Railroad

They traveled by night. They had only the North Star to guide them. For the people who escaped slavery on the Underground Railroad, darkness kept danger at bay. The dark was a friend. It kept the **bounty hunters** away. It kept the dogs and the guns away.

The Best Path to Freedom
Enslaved people desperate for freedom had two choices. They could try to escape on their own. They could also use the Underground Railroad. The Underground Railroad was the best-known path to freedom. It was set up in the 1780s by Quakers, and it helped tens of thousands of enslaved people to escape to freedom.

The escapees planned their path by thinking of people who could help them. They traveled between farms, called "stations." Those traveling on the railroad also stopped in towns where networks of people had been set up. The people who helped were called "conductors." Sometimes they were whites who held a deep belief that slavery was wrong. At other times, free African Americans aided the travelers.

U.S. History:
The Underground Railroad

Once escapees arrived at a safe place, they were given food and a bed. Then they were hidden. The next night they continued their journey. At each spot, they were directed to the next haven.

Some enslaved people traveled to free Northern states. The Underground Railroad might take an escapee to a border town such as Wilmington, Delaware. Delaware was a slave state. Beyond it was New Jersey. That state was free. Another popular destination was Canada. No slavery was allowed there. At places such as Buffalo, New York, escapees were able to travel across water to Canada. Once there, they were free.

Freedom for All

Some conductors on the Underground Railroad became famous for their courage and determination. Harriet Tubman is one example. When she was young, Tubman was enslaved. She escaped to the North. Then she began leading others to freedom. She made 19 journeys, leading 300 escapees to Canada and to freedom.

Harriet Tubman

The Underground Railroad helped many people escape slavery. In addition, it aided the cause of freedom for all enslaved people. People working for the Underground Railroad helped whites in the North understand the agony of slavery. Whites increasingly refused to obey such laws as the Fugitive Slave Act. This act forced escapees to return to slavery. Stories of the terrible lives of enslaved people made some whites in the North turn their backs on people who supported slavery.

The success of the Underground Railroad helped lead to the Civil War. More and more people in the North refused to return enslaved people to slavery. Southerners, in turn, passed more laws to force people to capture and return escapees. Most people in the South were furious about being told that their way of life was wrong. The rage and fury people felt about slavery in both the North and the South helped fuel the Civil War.

Strategy Tip

Because there is a photo of Harriet Tubman, you can assume she's an important figure in the selection. What information about Tubman can you add to your PLAN graphic?

When you finish the selection, look back at your PLAN graphic. Add the main points and the supporting information you need to understand the selection. Once you are satisfied you understand what you read, use a review technique such as writing a summary or making a list to review what you've learned about the Underground Railroad.

Apply It. . . . . To check your understanding of the selection, circle the best answer to each of the following questions.

1. The main idea of this selection is that
   a. Harriet Tubman was a famous conductor on the Underground Railroad.
   b. the Underground Railroad was the main cause of the Civil War.
   c. the Underground Railroad was an important way for people to escape slavery.
   d. both b and c

2. A *station* on the Underground Railroad was
   a. a place where escapees could safely rest.
   b. Canada, where slavery was illegal.
   c. an actual railroad station where escapees could catch a train to Canada or a free state.
   d. a new home for escapees.

Test Tip

Question 3 asks what the word *haven* means. Read the sentence and substitute each possible definition for the word *haven*. See which choice makes sense in the sentence.

3. The word *haven* in the section "The Best Path to Freedom" means
   a. a farm.
   b. a safe place.
   c. a plantation.
   d. a border state.

4. The Underground Railroad helped
   a. enslaved people earn their rights.
   b. enslaved people gain their freedom.
   c. people in the North understand the agony of slavery.
   d. both b and c

5. You can infer that the Fugitive Slave Act
   a. allowed enslaved people to go to free states.
   b. helped Southerners return escapees to slavery.
   c. was supported by the North.
   d. was never enforced.

Use the lines below to write your answers for numbers 6 and 7. Use your PLAN graphic to help you.

6. Describe a danger that slaves who escaped faced on their journey to freedom.

Escapees faced the dangers of bounty hunters, guns, and dogs.

7. What can you infer about Harriet Tubman from reading this selection?

Sample answer: You can infer that Harriet Tubman was intelligent and determined. You can also infer that she was brave because she escaped slavery and helped others gain their freedom as well.

U.S. History:
Lesson 10 America's Secret Weapon in World War II

Understand It...... This history article tells a story about a group of heroes of World War II. The PLAN strategy should help you understand the article because you can choose the graphic that works best for you. First, preview this article to find out how it is organized. If you think it's written in chronological, or time, order, use a sequence chart. If you think it compares and contrasts two things, use a Venn diagram. If it focuses on one topic, a wheel-and-spoke diagram could be your best choice. Once you decide how the article is organized, you can choose the graphic you think best fits it.

Try It............. Remember that when you use the PLAN strategy, you predict what the main points of the article might be. Below you'll find three possible PLAN graphics. You can use one of them or create a graphic of your own. Remember to make your graphic large enough so you can add notes. Do the first three steps of the PLAN method: predict, locate information, and add key words. If you find the graphic you've chosen doesn't work, try another graphic.

Strategy Tip
When you create a graphic, you may get halfway into it and realize it doesn't work. Don't keep going. Try another type of graphic.

America's Secret Weapon in World War II

The time was World War II. The United States was fighting Japan, and the U.S. Marines had a difficult problem. They had to find a way to keep their communications secret. Japan kept breaking the U.S. codes. An order would go out: Attack there. The Japanese would pick up the message on their radios and decipher the code. They knew their enemy's plan, so they had time to prepare.

The Americans became desperate as the Japanese broke code after code. Then Philip Johnson went to the Marines. He had an idea. Johnson had grown up on a Navajo reservation. He knew the language, and he knew it was very hard to learn. Fewer than 30 non-Navajos knew it. None of them were Japanese.

A New Idea
Johnson thought Navajo could work well as a code for several reasons. Navajo is unwritten. It has no alphabet. It is very complex. A word spoken in four different ways can have four different meanings. The Marine officer was not sure about Johnson's idea. Even so, he agreed to give it a try. The Marines had to try *something*.

Johnson set up a test. He showed what could be done in 20 seconds. The Navajos could encode, transmit, and decode a three-line message. The officer was impressed. The machines that did the job took a half hour. The Marines brought in two of their code breakers. The code breakers didn't even know how to write down what they were hearing. Trying to translate it was impossible. The Navajo **Code Talkers** had a job. The officer ordered 200 Navajos to be trained for code-talking duty.

In May 1942, the first 29 recruits created the Navajo code. It was based on the Navajo language. The code could not be understood by a native speaker who was not trained, though. The code included words created to represent military terms. For example, *submarine* became "iron fish." The Navajos memorized the code. Then 27 Code Talkers were sent to the Pacific. Two stayed behind to teach new recruits. Before the war was over, 400 Navajos had served as Code Talkers.

Their success has become legendary. The system was simple. Two Code Talkers talked to each other. They passed on information about where troops were going. They explained what was happening. And they **frustrated** the Japanese. The Japanese broke the Army and Navy codes. The Marine code remained unbroken.

Making a Name

The Code Talkers made their name at Iwo Jima, where one of the most important battles of the war was fought. In that battle, 4,189 Americans were killed and 15,308 were injured. On the Japanese side, 22,000 were killed.

During the first two days of the battle, six Code Talkers worked around the clock. They coded 800 messages. Not one was wrong. Major Howard Connor was the signal officer for that battle. "Were it not for the Navajos," he said, "the Marines would never have taken Iwo Jima."

In 1968, the Marines finally told the Code Talkers' story. It had been a classified secret until then. When a high-ranking Japanese official found out about the Code Talkers, he said, "Thank you. That is a puzzle I thought would never be solved."

In 1983, President Ronald Reagan honored the Code Talkers. In 1992, the Pentagon set up an exhibit that shows the history of the code. The Code Talkers have gradually gained the respect they deserve.

Vocabulary Tip

Code Talkers is a compound word. You know what the parts of the word mean, though, so you can figure out the meaning.

Vocabulary Tip

What does the word *frustrated* mean in this sentence? Think about the sentences around it. How might the Japanese have felt if they were unable to break this one code?

After you read, note what you learned. Revise your PLAN graphic if you need to. Then review your work to make sure you understand what you have read.

U.S. History:
America's Secret Weapon in World War II

Apply It. . . . . To check your understanding of this article, circle the best answer to each of the following questions.

1. Philip Johnson thought the Navajo language would work as a code because
   a. Navajo words can have several different meanings.
   b. Navajo is a very complex language with no alphabet.
   c. the Navajo language was known by the Japanese.
   (d.) both a and b

2. Military officials were not sure about using the Navajo code because
   a. they thought there were not enough native Navajo speakers.
   (b.) they didn't know if it would work.
   c. they didn't know how to write it down.
   d. they thought the Japanese could easily break it.

Test Tip

Turn back to the first paragraph of the article. Reread the sentence about deciphering the code. Now substitute each choice in question 3 in that sentence. Which choice makes sense?

3. The phrase *decipher the code* in the first paragraph means
   (a.) figure out the code.
   b. change the code.
   c. adjust the code.
   d. replace the code.

4. The main point of this article is that
   a. the Navajo Code Talkers fought bravely in World War II.
   (b.) the Navajo Code Talkers created an unbreakable code in World War II.
   c. the Code Talkers did not get the recognition they deserved.
   d. the Japanese admitted they lost the war because of the Code Talkers.

5. The code the Navajo Code Talkers used
   a. translated Navajo into English.
   b. could be understood by any Navajo.
   (c.) was based on the Navajo language.
   d. is still used in military communications.

Use the lines below to write your answers for numbers 6 and 7. You can use your PLAN notes to help you.

6. How did the Navajo Code Talkers frustrate the Japanese?

Sample answer: The Code Talkers frustrated the Japanese because they could not figure out how to break the code. One example was at Iwo Jima, when Code Talkers were responsible for the Marines winning that battle.

7. Summarize the story of how the Navajo Code Talkers came to exist.

First, Philip Johnson came up with the idea. He brought it to the Marines. The Marines tested it, decided it would work, and recruited Navajos to create the code. Then more Navajos were trained to use it.

Lesson 11   Civics: The "Glory That Was Greece"

Understand It...... The PLAN strategy will work best to help you understand this article. Read the article. Then decide what graphic you will use.

Try It............. Preview the article to predict what you think you will learn. Below, you will find three possible PLAN graphics. Use one of them or create a graphic of your own. As you fill in your graphic, do the first three steps of PLAN, which are predict, locate, and add key words. Add check marks next to subjects you know about. Add question marks next to subjects you do not know much about. Note supporting information after you have read the article.

Strategy Tip

Sketch different graphics as you preview the selection. You may find that the second or third one fits the selection better than the first one you try.

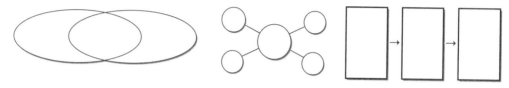

Vocabulary Tip

In social studies texts, terms like *city–states* are often followed by definitions.

The "Glory That Was Greece"

When people talk about ancient Greece, they often speak of the "glory that was Greece." This is because many people think that the government of ancient Greece was the first one to use democracy.

Greece's origins date back to about 1900 B.C. The early Greeks were nomadic herders. They roamed from place to place to find good pastures for their animals. Then people began to settle in one place, forming **city–states**. Each city–state had a separate government. Ancient Greece was not a unified nation. Instead, Greek citizens were loyal to the cities they lived in. These city–states were small. Athens was the only city–state with more than 20,000 residents.

The government of a city–state generally went through several stages.

- **The Age of Kings**. In early times, the ruler was a rich landowner who acted as a king. That system lasted until about the 8th and 7th centuries B.C.

- **Oligarchy** (rule of the few). Wealthy landowners who ruled together made up an oligarchy. Often, though, everyone else was unhappy. In addition, the landowners often quarreled among themselves.

- **Tyranny**. When people who were ruled by an oligarchy became very unhappy, one of the rulers would promise relief. Then he would seize power. Today, *tyrant* has a negative meaning. A tyrant is a person who rules without the permission of the people. In ancient Greece, though, a tyrant was simply a ruler who was not born into a royal family.

Civics:
The "Glory That Was Greece"

Strategy Tip

When you see a list with words in bold type or bullets (dots), you can assume the information is important. Add this information to your PLAN chart.

- **Beginnings of Democracy**. Often, a tyrant told his subjects they should have a voice in decisions. The idea became common in many city–states. The city–state of Athens led the way. By the 5th century B.C., Athens was the world's first democracy. In a democracy, lawmakers are elected by the people.

The Glories of Athens

When people speak of the wonders of ancient Greece, they usually mean Athens. Athens's rulers realized that a strong navy was the key to success. Athens controlled a large area with its ships. This meant the city–state had plenty of tax money. Athens's citizens got the benefits. The city was filled with sculpture and paintings. Education had been only for a few rich people. It soon became available to many.

However, Athens had a side that was not glorious. The miseries of enslaved people helped make the rich life possible for Athenians. Historians estimate that one-fourth to four-fifths of the people living in Athens were enslaved. Many enslaved people had been defeated in war. Others were simply captured. Some enslaved people were able to buy their freedom. Many, however, lived terrible lives.

Because the citizens of Athens had enslaved people to do their work, they had plenty of extra time. Athenians painted and wrote. People who are trying to find food to eat do not have those choices. This meant that Athenians had the time to produce remarkable ideas about philosophy and government.

In Athens, every citizen could vote, but not everyone could be a citizen. Women, enslaved people, and people from outside Athens could not be citizens. Every ten days, the Assembly of Citizens met. At least 6,000 citizens attended each meeting. If they failed to come, police rounded them up.

At the assembly, any citizen could speak. A council of 500 was chosen every year by lottery. The council chose the topics to be discussed. The council also ran the city. Citizens took turns being generals and judges.

Being a citizen in Athens had its dangers. Once a year, the Assembly handed out broken pieces of pottery. If a citizen wanted to **exile** someone, he scratched the person's name on the pottery. If more than 6,000 voters agreed, the man was **exiled** from Athens for ten years.

The End of the Glory

Envy and ambition caused the end of Athens's glory days. As Athens gained power, neighboring city–states grew fearful. Finally, in 431 B.C., the struggle that ended Athens's power began. The war pitted the naval power of Athens against the land power of Sparta, another large

Vocabulary Tip

Sometimes, an unfamiliar word appears more than once, as *exile* does here. By comparing the different ways the word is used in context, you can guess at its meaning.

city–state. In the first part of the war, Athens struck at its enemies from the sea, refusing to fight on land. However, a deadly plague struck Athens, killing one-fourth of its residents. One of the dead was Pericles, the leader of Athens. The city drifted like a ship without a captain.

The next leader, Alcibiades, dreamed of fame as an army leader. He began a great land attack. The Athenian army was destroyed. Its soldiers were enslaved. In 404 B.C., Athens became part of Sparta. Sparta's traditions were not as democratic as those of Athens. The glory days of ancient Greece were over.

After you have finished reading the article, review your PLAN chart. Use the chart to write a summary of the article.

Apply It........... To check your understanding of the article, circle the best answer to each question below.

1. Which of these was *not* true of the Athenian Assembly?
   a. Enslaved people were not allowed to vote.
   b. Any citizen could speak.
   c. The council was chosen by lottery.
   (d.) The Assembly began in Sparta.

2. Athens lost its democracy after Sparta won the war in 404 B.C. because
   a. Sparta wanted to teach Athens a lesson.
   b. all Athenians were enslaved.
   (c.) Sparta used a different system of government.
   d. Athenians realized that democracy had made them weak.

3. Athens's navy was important in its history because
   (a.) it allowed Athens to control a large area, collect taxes, and become rich.
   b. the commanders of the navy were also the city's leaders.
   c. it allowed the navy to make money for Athens through trade.
   d. the navy wanted a democracy.

4. In the first section of the article, *oligarchy* refers to
   a. a citizen of Athens.
   b. a system of government in which every citizen has a vote.
   (c.) a system of government in which a few people have power.
   d. the government of Sparta.

5. Athens fell because
   a. the people had become lazy from not working hard.
   (b.) it lost a war to Sparta.
   c. its enslaved people rebelled.
   d. the citizens did not want to fight.

Civics:
The "Glory That Was Greece"

Use the lines below to write your answers for numbers 6 and 7. You can use your PLAN notes and your summary to help you.

6. Think about the democracy we have in the United States today. How would you compare and contrast democracy in the United States to democracy in ancient Athens?

Sample answer: The democracies are the same because both have citizens who vote and representatives who make decisions. They are different because many more people can hold citizenship today.

Test Tip

Question 7 asks for evidence. When you give evidence, you need to write facts and details from the article.

7. Why did having a lot of spare time lead ancient Athens to develop a "glorious" civilization? Give evidence from the article to support your answer.

Historians refer to the "glory" of Athens because its people had the leisure to think, to write, to paint, to create sculptures, and to create democracy.

Lesson 12   Sociology: Living at the Mall

Understand It...... This article is about the role of the modern shopping mall in U.S. society. You probably know a few things about shopping malls. Try the PLAN strategy with this reading because it works well when you are familiar with the topic. You should be able to preview the article and make predictions about the kind of information you will learn.

Try It............. Below are three graphic organizers for PLAN charts. When you use the PLAN strategy, you begin by reviewing the article. Then you decide which graphic works best for you. Once you have made that decision, add information to it from your reading. Finally, note your understanding of what you have read by writing a summary.

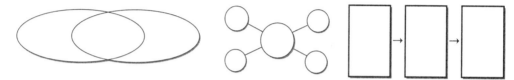

Strategy Tip
When you preview, you add what you learn to what you already know to make predictions.

Strategy Tip
Think about the subheadings. What do you know about these topics? Use this information to predict what you will learn. You can also use the subheadings to review.

Living at the Mall

Shopping malls are a part of almost every community. Once people spent time at the town square or on Main Street. Today, the shopping mall is the new town square.

For many decades, a town square surrounded by shops was the center of many communities. The lawns and sidewalks and parks also belonged to the community. Such spaces included not only stores but also post offices, community and government offices, libraries, and, perhaps, a town auditorium. Town squares became centers because people went there for many reasons, from mailing packages to returning library books. Along the way, they met neighbors. People stopped and discussed news, community issues, and national affairs. Town squares often served as centers for other community events, such as band concerts or holiday ceremonies.

The History of the Shopping Center
Then along came the shopping center. Since the 1920s, when the idea of a central shopping area first developed, shopping-center design has gone through several stages. The first stage, which appeared in California in the 1920s and 1930s, was the result of a new invention: the car. Developers bought a piece of land, provided plenty of parking spaces, and grouped together several stores.

In the 1950s and 1960s, shopping malls grew with the suburbs. In most cases, suburbs had no town squares. Suburbs often had no large groups of stores. Developers created larger groups of stores. By then, however, planners had had time to do some thinking about the

Sociology:
Living at the Mall

arrangement of stores. Developers knew that a major department store or two would attract customers. Those stores could be at either end of an area that housed many smaller stores. To get from one major store to the other, shoppers would have to walk past many smaller stores.

These malls were quite different from town squares. In towns, store owners often owned the land their stores were built on. Shopping centers changed that. A developer owned all the land and made all the rules. The developer often set hours for the stores, chose the tenants, and enforced rules about how stores could look.

Stores in the first shopping centers all had outside entrances but often faced inward as well. This inward side was a small self-contained world. Shopping center owners didn't want shoppers to think about the world outside. They wanted people to focus on shopping, and people did.

Enclosed malls **disconnected** people from the outside world even more. People inside an air-conditioned mall didn't need to think about the world outside. They only needed to concentrate on the opportunity to spend money.

In recent years, developers have followed the trend to create "shopping experiences." In Colorado, one Denver mall calls itself a "retail resort." From cozy leather chairs to wooden log walls, the design says "dude ranch." However, this dude ranch is entirely devoted to shopping, not to the great outdoors.

Should Malls Be More Than Just Stores?

As small towns saw their main streets die and as suburban residents wondered where their childhood meeting places had gone, complaints about malls grew. Malls were soulless places devoted to greed instead of to the common good. Malls told young people that the best place to be was a place where they could spend money.

Some planners and community activists say it is too late to save many downtowns. They think that the mall serves the same purpose as the town square did.

Dr. Judith Coady, a professor at the University of Connecticut, told *The New York Times* that she began to study shopping malls as community centers. She found out that she was wrong. "I expected to find the mall as some kind of new community," she said. "But I found that the mall is not a community at all. . . . The focus is on consumption, on the pleasure of just being there. The issues that are part of our everyday community are not discussed there, so it isn't a community."

Vocabulary Tip

You can understand *disconnected* by looking at the parts of the word. The prefix *dis-* means "the opposite of." The base word *connect* means "to join." The suffix *-ed* shows that something happened in the past. So *disconnected* means "not joined."

Coady watched people at the mall and found that they walked differently inside than they did outside. "It's a slower walk to the rhythm of music in the mall," she said. "The eyes are unfocused. Generally speaking, there's a kind of glaze in the eyes. The mall brings it on."

Because people are with others in the mall, she said that they feel like they are part of a community. "However, as people wander in the malls," she said, "community problems get worse. While people are dallying in the malls, the problems remain hidden and out of sight." Some planners are trying to build suburbs based on a town square design, but much of America meets at malls. Can malls become more than just huge groups of stores?

The Walt Whitman Center at Rutgers University is working on a project to turn shopping malls into more active areas of communities. It is bringing new elements to malls, such as community theaters, public-health centers, day-care centers, public libraries, or playgrounds. "If malls are the only public spaces left to us in many parts of the country, they must become more like real towns," the project leaders wrote. "If business is not to become the **sole** public activity we engage in, we must offer alternative activities—civic, cultural, athletic, political, and recreational—that define us as citizens as well as consumers."

Developers and mall owners who are happy with the way malls are may not want to add those elements. Some developers, though, welcome the idea. A mall in Massachusetts has a library, a church, and a home for senior citizens. In Silver Spring, Maryland, a developer is creating a mall that will serve as a town square. It will continue to bring people together in a place where they feel safe. At the same time, they can enjoy themselves and various recreational activities.

The future mall may be different from today's malls. Imagine a mall that serves as a town square, where people meet to talk, check out library books, and listen to debates and concerts. The mall we have known for decades does not have to be the mall of the future.

Vocabulary Tip

The word *sole* has several different meanings—"a fish," "the bottom of a shoe," and "only." You can figure out which one fits by looking at the rest of the sentence.

After you finish adding information to your PLAN chart, look over what you have written. Add other important ideas or details. Then write a summary of the article. That will help you remember what you have read.

Sociology:
Living at the Mall

Apply It . . . . To check your understanding of the article, circle the best answer to each question below.

1. The main idea of this article is that
    (a.) shopping malls have replaced town squares.
    b. shopping malls are good places to shop.
    c. shopping malls are becoming larger and larger.
    d. both b and c

2. According to the article, developers began enclosing malls because
    (a.) they didn't want customers to think about the outside world
    b. they did not want customers to feel uncomfortable.
    c. the store owners demanded it.
    d. they wanted to make shopping pleasant.

3. " 'However, as these people wander in the malls,' she said, 'community problems get worse. While people are dallying in the malls, the problems remain hidden and out of sight.' " In this passage, the word *dallying* means
    (a.) spending time.
    b. working.
    c. hiding out.
    d. eating.

4. Judith Coady learned through her research that
    a. malls serve as community centers.
    b. people want malls to be more like community centers.
    c. developers plan to make malls more like community centers.
    (d.) people at malls incorrectly feel they are part of a community.

5. Developers might not want a mall to be more like a town square because
    (a.) developers might not want to spend money to change the mall.
    b. people might not come to the mall.
    c. developers would not want disagreements in the mall.
    d. developers would not want to give out social services.

Use the lines below to write your answers for numbers 6 and 7. Use your PLAN chart to help you.

Test Tip

Question 6 has two parts. You must tell *both* how town squares and shopping malls are the same and how they are different.

6. How are town squares and shopping malls similar? How are they different?

Sample answer: Properties in the center of older communities tend to be owned by different people. They are outside and in the middle of town, and they have a variety of functions besides shopping. Shopping malls are only for shopping, are owned by one company, and are usually enclosed. Both are places where people meet or at least see one another.

7. What is the author's opinion of malls? Use examples from the article to support your ideas.

Sample answer: The author is trying to present both sides of the argument about whether shopping malls can or should function as community meeting places. She mentions complaints people have about malls, ways people use malls, a study that shows that people in malls are not part of a community, and efforts by developers to include space for noncommercial activities.

Unit 3 Review: **PLAN**

In this unit, you have practiced using the PLAN reading strategy. Use this strategy when you read the selection below. Use a separate sheet of paper to draw a chart, take notes, and summarize what you learn.

Hint *Remember that all reading strategies have activities for before, during, and after reading. To review these steps, look at the inside back cover of this book.*

Mapping North America

The first maps of North America were those made by Native Americans. These maps were made on bone, on bark, on wood, and on rock.

The maps had different purposes than those of the explorers. Native Americans' maps were made for local use. They showed the locations of wars or where ancient groups had lived. Other maps showed the routes between villages. Maps might also show where family groups lived or where holy places were.

Many of the first large-scale maps of North America were made by explorers. They wanted to direct others to North America. They also wanted to show where they had been.

The First Maps of the Americas

The first known map by an outsider is from 1500. It is a Spanish map that shows part of North America. It was drawn by Juan de la Cosa, who may have sailed with Columbus.

Maps of the Americas began to appear around the time of Christopher Columbus, in 1492. In some of these maps, North and South America are divided by a large ocean. In others, a river travels across Canada and connects the Pacific and Atlantic Oceans.

Another of the continuing errors in mapmaking came from one repeated mistake. In map after map, California is shown as a huge island. It took a 1747 statement by the King of Spain that California was *not* an island to clear up that confusion.

When countries began to establish colonies, maps of another sort began to appear. These maps showed where the colonies were. That was important for supply ships.

In the 18th century, France and Britain needed maps for military use. They were fighting each other in the colonies. Then the British wanted good maps to use in the war against the colonists.

Mapping the West

Those living in America began making their own maps for the war. They also made maps of their

Unit 3 Review: PLAN

settlements. In the 19th century, mapmakers mapped the West.

When the 1800s began, there was little knowledge of the middle of the country. There were settlements in the West, and the East was fairly well mapped. The center, though, was known only by Native Americans. One explorer reported that the middle of the country was nothing but desert.

Another push to map the West came with the railroads. To lay tracks to cross the country, railroad companies needed good maps.

By the early 1900s, North America was fully mapped. However, there are still surprises. Even in the 1980s, remote sensors on satellites were finding tiny islands in the Canadian Arctic.

Use your notes and charts to help you answer the questions below.

1. Native American maps differed from the maps of explorers because
   - **a.** Native Americans needed maps for different reasons.
   - **b.** Native Americans did not understand the purpose of maps.
   - **c.** Europeans did not know much about maps.
   - **d.** both b and c

2. Europeans used North American maps in the 18th century to
   - **a.** mark a country's boundaries.
   - **b.** plan battles.
   - **c.** help explorers reach America.
   - **d.** help trappers find animals.

3. Which is a reason the West was mapped?
   - **a.** to find a route for the Revolutionary Army.
   - **b.** to find the best place to put railroad tracks.
   - **c.** to help the Europeans fight the Native Americans.
   - **d.** to find new sources of gold.

4. Summarize the important points of this article.

   Maps were used for many reasons, including military use, informing supply ships where to go, and the development of railroads.

5. What might be the effects of believing an error in a map, such as that the American West was only desert?

   Sample answer: Believing an error on a map could falsely indicate that there is no civilization in an area. It could also cause military troops to lose their way during battle.

Unit 4 Strategy: PACA

Understand It...... PACA stands for **P**redicting **A**nd **C**onfirming **A**ctivity. Active readers often make a few predictions about an article's topic. While they read, they look for information that will confirm their predictions. The PACA strategy can help make you an active reader, too. It can help you think about what you read.

Try It............. PACA is a good strategy to use when you know something about a topic. You preview the reading, form some ideas about the topic, and make some predictions. Then you read to see whether your predictions are right. If they're wrong, you revise them. You'll probably also find some ideas that you didn't expect.

The article on the next page is about in-line skating. You probably know something about in-line skating. You might have seen people skate. You might have skated yourself. Use what you know to make some predictions about the article. Follow along with a student as he uses the PACA strategy.

Strategy Tip
Base your predictions on *why* you are reading. For example, if you are reading a social studies assignment, your predictions will be different from those you'd make when you are reading a science assignment.

Step 1. Predict what you might learn in the article.

Preview the article to get an idea of what it is about. The student looked at the title, which told him the article was about in-line skating. When he read the subheadings, he knew the article would contain information about safety and basic skills. The student thought about what he already knew about in-line skating. Then he previewed the article. Here is what he thought:

What do I know about in-line skating? I see kids doing it. They seem to really like it. It looks like a cross between ice skating and roller skating. Some skaters go very fast. How do they stay in control?

The student then wrote his predictions in the Predictions column of his PACA chart. Use the PACA chart below to add your own predictions about the article. What other information might the article contain? Use what you know about in-line skating and what you see as you preview the article.

Predictions	Support
the article will talk about the history of in-line skating	
how to skate in races	
how to skate safely	
learn the basics of in-line skating	

PACA

Step 2. Read, then confirm your predictions.

First, read the article. Then look at your PACA chart. When you confirm a prediction, make a check mark in the small box next to that prediction. When you find points you did not predict, write them. Then draw a star in the box by each new prediction. If your predictions were wrong, revise them or cross them out. Here's how the student began reading and marking the predictions he made:

Predictions	Support
the article will talk about the history of in-line skating ✓	
~~how to skate in races~~ * how to skate safely	

Strategy Tip
As you write your predictions, leave plenty of space to add points you did not expect.

In Step with In-Line Skating

In 1760, Joseph Merlin decided to attach wooden spools to the bottoms of his shoes. That way, he thought, he could skate in the summer when there was no ice. Merlin's idea worked fairly well—until he skated into an expensive mirror, shattering it.

The in-line skates of today are much more than wooden spools on a shoe. The in-line skating story of this century began in 1980. That year, two Minnesota brothers tried to figure out a way to practice ice hockey in the summer. They invented the first modern in-line skates.

The idea caught on quickly. By the mid-1990s, in-line skating was *in*. At the start of the 21st century, the sport is still growing. More than six million skaters swoop and glide across paved areas everywhere. If you want to try the sport, however, you need to keep a few things in mind. Think about the equipment you need and about learning to skate safely. Most skaters recommend that you take a couple of lessons before risking your knees—or your neck.

How do you choose skates? The most important factors are the outer boot, the inner boot, and the wheels. The outer boot needs to be stiff enough to support your ankles, especially if you are a beginner. The inner boot should let your foot breathe and feel comfortable. A slight rubbing in the store can mean big blisters on the road.

You'll have to make some decisions about the wheels. First, you need to decide how many wheels you want. Most skates have four wheels. Racing models have five wheels—on those skates, expect to *fly*. Your skates may have only three wheels if you have small feet. The size of the wheels matters, too. The smaller the wheel, the slower you will go. Most adults choose wheels from 70 to 72 mm (millimeters) in diameter. Children's wheels may be as small as 64 mm. Racers, who need speed, may go to 80 mm in diameter.

Safety First

Safety is a big issue for in-line skaters. Skaters can move very quickly, and it's easy to wind up on the concrete. No one can promise you won't fall. If you wear the right gear, though, you can avoid serious injury. Along with your skates, you need to buy wrist guards, knee and elbow pads, and a helmet.

The wrist guards help prevent the most common in-line skating injuries: broken and sprained wrists. When you fall, you will probably tumble forward. If you can, get your hands out of the way. However, your instinct will be to try to break your

An in-line skater in protective gear soars above a curved ramp.

fall with your wrists. Wrist guards can **minimize** an injury. Knee guards and elbow pads provide the same kind of protection for falls involving knees and elbows.

Wearing a helmet when you skate is as important as wearing a helmet when you ride a bike. Head injuries can be very serious—even fatal. A helmet can prevent or minimize injuries to your head. *Always* wear one. It's that simple.

Blading Basics

The basics of in-line skating are easy to learn. In-line skating is more like ice skating than roller skating. Some people think in-line skating is an easier sport to learn and a lot more fun. When you first try the sport, find a flat, smooth surface such as a parking lot. (Make sure skating is allowed there.) The skating surface should be surrounded by grass, not gravel or dirt. If you need to slow down or can't remember how to stop, you can jump on the grass.

PACA

As in ice skating, you move forward by pushing one foot off to the side. Then you shift your weight to the other leg and push off. Soon you'll find a rhythm, a kind of glide. You also need to learn to stop. Extend your arms for better balance. Push down the heel of your right foot, bending your knees as you do. The brake on your heel will slow you down. Once you're comfortable, you can try fancier ways of stopping.

Consider taking a clinic on blading. Even if you know the basics, you might find an advanced clinic helpful. Learning the tricks of the best skaters can make in-line skating even more fun.

Step 3. Support your predictions with details.

After you finish adding or revising your predictions, look at what you wrote. Each prediction needs details to support it. Write the evidence in the Support column. Here is how the student added to his predictions:

Predictions		Support
the article will talk about the history of in-line skating	✓	first skates in 1760, modern skates in 1980
~~how to skate in races~~ how to skate safely	*	first, find flat pavement or concrete, use side to side gliding motion
learn the basics of in-line skating	✓	similar to ice skating—need to learn how to start, stop

Now go back to your predictions. Fill in details in the Support column that will help you remember the main points of the article. When you're finished, keep your PACA chart. You can use it to help you review for a test.

Apply It............ Try the PACA strategy with a reading assignment you have. First, preview the assignment and write some predictions about it on a PACA chart. Next, read the assignment. After you read, look for information about the predictions you made. When you find them, add check marks to the small box. When you see points you did not predict, add them to your chart and add stars in the small box. Finally, go back and write the evidence or examples that support each prediction. Your notes should be a good review of the important points in your assignment.

Lesson 13

World History: Caught in the Blitz

Understand It...... Look at the headline and photograph that appear with this letter. Then preview the letter. You'll probably have a good idea of what the subject is: World War II. You may know some things about World War II. Because all these things can give you clues to what you might read, the PACA strategy can help you get the most from this letter.

Try It............. Draw a PACA chart like the one below on a separate sheet of paper. After you preview the letter, make your predictions. The writer put an address and a date on the letter, so you know where and when it was written. Look closely at the photo. Does it give you an idea about what "the Blitz" was? You can probably predict that a *blitz* is a very destructive event.

Now read the letter. After you read, review your predictions. Add a check mark in the small box if you can confirm a prediction. If you find information you didn't predict, write it in the Predictions column and add a star to the small box. Cross out or revise predictions that were wrong. Then write the evidence for your predictions in the Support column.

Strategy Tip

You might not be able to make many predictions about this reading. Thinking about predictions, whether you can make any or not, makes you more aware of the subject. Make sure, though, that you note the important facts you did not predict.

Predictions	Support

Caught in the Blitz

London, England
May 13, 1941

Dear Jimmy,

I've been so involved in my troubles. But until I got your note from Boston, I didn't realize how worried you might be about what's going on here. Our school days together seem so long ago. I have so much to say that I hardly know where to start. Perhaps the easiest way is to start at the beginning: September 7, 1940. That's when it all began.

You probably know that Hitler decided to start bombing London then. He figured he could easily bring us to our knees. He didn't—or at least he hasn't yet. If things don't change soon, though, I don't know what will happen.

I remember the shock of hearing the **drone** of the planes from far away and then hearing the explosions. They seemed endless. Mum,

Vocabulary Tip

Although you might not know the word *drone* in this sentence, you can guess that a *drone* is a sound.

World History: Caught in the Blitz

Dad, Jenny, and I had taken shelter in a closet on the ground floor of our house. We could still hear the sounds, though.

At the end of that first night, I came out of the house just as dawn was breaking. All around me was rubble. The day before, there had been flower boxes and tidy stores and buildings—and now, nothing. Piles of silent bricks, glass everywhere, and pieces of broken walls that were jagged and smoking. The other thing I remember, besides the unbelievable destruction, was the sound—or lack of it. The city was almost totally silent, particularly right at dawn. I found out the Germans had dropped 600 *tons* of bombs on London that night.

The next night, it was the same, and the next and the next. We started spending the night in the Underground, after the trains had stopped for the day. One problem with staying there was the people all around us. Some acted crazy. One man just started cackling one night, and no one could get him to stop. Sleep was impossible.

After a while, people began calling the nightly bombings "the Blitz." What strikes me is how we got used to it. You can get used to just about anything. For the next two months, Hitler bombed us—*every single night.* Everyone knew someone who had died. Whole families decided not to take shelter or were homeless or had lost people. I could see why people didn't take shelter. The lines to get into the Underground stations began forming early in the day. After a while, I thought, "Well, what will happen will happen. I could just as easily get hit here." Of course, it wasn't true, but the longer it went on, the more we started thinking, "Well, nothing has happened so far, so. . . ."

One night, we decided to stay in our house. I don't think any of us slept all night. The whining of the airplanes was terrible. My stomach felt like one big knot. The sound just wouldn't go away. Then the orange would light the sky, and I'd sometimes see flames.

The bombing went on and on, and although I never got used to the sound of the whining planes, we started pretending that nothing was happening. We even started going out at night.

Officials examine extensive damage caused by a WWII bombing in London.

We found a restaurant we really liked. We could go there and forget what was happening. They played loud music. I suppose that was to cover up the sounds outside.

Strategy Tip

As you preview, look for terms within quotation marks. Here, quotation marks surround the term "the Blitz." What information have you noticed so far about this terrible time?

Strategy Tip

What does this photograph show you about the Blitz? Add a prediction to your PACA chart about what the Blitz was like.

One night, a bomb hit the restaurant. It seemed like it had fallen right on my head. I have to try to describe it for you. It might be good for me. I've really tried not to think about it, but I dream about it.

One minute, we were partying and then nothing—blackness. The explosion knocked me out. When I came to, I was confused. I couldn't figure out why I was slumped on the floor, covered with dust, and where the walls had gone. I couldn't understand why I was not moving. I felt sticky. It was completely quiet. Then I saw a flame nearby and another, and suddenly I knew what was happening. We'd been hit.

The stickiness was blood. It was all over my shirt. I just sat there, looking at it. I had no desire to move. I felt like I was watching a movie. Of course, eventually ambulances and nurses came. They moved me to an open space outside where many other people were all laid out. Someone stitched up my arm. That was where the blood was coming from.

I'm fine now. I no longer think the bombs will stop falling. They never do. Three nights ago, more than 2,000 fires broke out across London. The drone was intense that night. I don't think I'll ever hear a plane again without looking for a place to hide.

Yours,

Jeremy

When you finish reading the letter, look over your PACA chart. Did you find information that confirmed your predictions? If not, revise your predictions or add new ones. Clear PACA notes can help you review the important points the writer of the letter made.

Apply It. . . . . To check your understanding of the letter, circle the best answer to each question below.

1. Jeremy wrote the letter to Jimmy to
   a. let Jimmy know he is fine.
   b. make his American friend feel sorry for him.
   c. explain what is happening during the Blitz.
   d. explain to Jimmy why his country is at war.

2. Jeremy thinks he will never be able to hear another plane without looking for a place to hide because
   a. it will remind him of London.
   b. it will remind him of listening to the German planes landing nearby.
   c. it will remind him how much he misses his friend.
   d. it will remind him of the bombings.

World History: Caught in the Blitz

Test Tip

Question 3 asks you for the meaning of a word. If you don't remember a definition, reread the selection. Seeing the word in context can help you define it.

3. In this letter, the *Underground* is
   a. a bomb shelter.
   b. a subway or transportation system.
   c. anywhere people can get away from the bombs.
   d. a basement.

4. Which choice best describes what Jeremy says at the end of the letter?
   a. He says that he wants to leave London.
   b. He says that his family was killed in the bombing.
   c. He says that he realizes the bombings will continue.
   d. He says that he is happy to still be with his family.

5. Jeremy tells about the bomb falling on the restaurant mainly because
   a. he thinks if he tells the story he won't have nightmares about it.
   b. he wants Jimmy to send food.
   c. he wants to tell Jimmy that the Blitz isn't that bad.
   d. he is trying to show Jimmy the terrible times he's seen.

Test Tip

Unless the directions tell you otherwise, answer short-answer questions in complete sentences.

Use the lines below to write your answers for numbers 6 and 7. You can use your PACA chart and your notes to help you.

6. What does the letter tell you about the relationship between Jeremy and Jimmy?

   Their relationship is friendly. They went to school together, and the writer writes as though the recipient is a good friend. They aren't that close, though, because the writer hasn't written to his friend in a long time.

7. What is the worst part of the Blitz for Jeremy? Explain your answer with examples from the letter.

   Sample answer: The worst part of the Blitz is the constant bombing, night after night. I think this because the writer keeps talking about how the bombing never ends.

Lesson 14

Geography: The Silk Road

Understand It...... This geography selection tells about a famous trade route in Asia called the Silk Road. The PACA strategy is a good one to use with this selection because the map offers a lot of information. Use this information to make predictions about the selection.

Try It............. Draw a PACA chart like the one below on another sheet of paper. Then preview the selection. As you preview, look at the title and the subheadings. Also look at the map. Use that information to write a few predictions in the Predictions column. Since you will be reading a geography selection, you might guess that some information will be about places or landforms. What do you predict the "Silk Road" will be?

After you read the selection, fill in your PACA chart. Remember to make a check mark next to each prediction that proved to be correct. When you see important information you did not predict, write that. Make a star next to these new points. In the Support column, write the evidence that supports or confirms each prediction. Cross out any incorrect predictions.

Strategy Tip

In a geography selection, *what* and *where* questions are important. However, ask a few *why* questions to be sure you understand the point of the reading.

Predictions	Support

Vocabulary Tip

You probably know *pass* as a verb, meaning "to go by something." Use that information to define *pass* as a noun. What might a mountain *pass* be?

The Silk Road

The mountain **passes** were terrifying. Avalanches and falling rocks were common. Most travelers avoided the great desert. At any moment, fierce bandits might strip travelers of all they owned. However, for 1,600 years, the 5,000-mile Silk Road was so important that traders risked all these dangers. The end of the road, they knew, meant wealth almost beyond measure.

The Silk Road runs between China and Europe. It became an active trade route about 100 B.C. For the first time, people in Europe and Asia could exchange goods. Most important, Europeans could transport their gold to China and bring back silk.

Europeans loved silk. The fabric reached Rome around the 1st century B.C. The Romans had no fabric as soft, as shimmering, or as fine. Almost instantly, silk became the favorite fabric of the rich. It was worth its weight in gold. The high price of Chinese silk made the dangers of the Silk Road a reasonable risk for traders.

Geography:
The Silk Road

Chinese silk makers soon realized they possessed a valuable trade secret. Silk making was almost unknown outside China. Silkworms spun cocoons. The silk makers carefully unraveled the cocoons into silken thread. They then wove the thread into silk cloth. The Chinese mastered the art of silk making.

From the Edge of Civilization

On its eastern end, the Silk Road began in Changan, the capital of the Chinese empire at the time. Today, Changan is called Xi'an. From Changan, caravans of camels set off for 500 miles along a fertile stretch of land to Dunhuang.

The Chinese considered Dunhuang to be the edge of civilization because, for the next 900 miles, the caravans had to cross the Tarim Basin. This basin is one of the most terrifying stretches of land on Earth. It is home to the Takla Makan, the driest desert in Asia. Sand dunes there have buried cities. Water is scarce. Travelers on the Silk Road hoped they would not have to face swirling sandstorms or terrible temperatures. These temperatures range from −4° F (−20° C) to 104° F (40° C).

At the end of Takla Makan, caravans faced the passes of the Pamir Mountains. The narrow, death-defying ledges, which are almost 15,000 feet (4,570 m) high, nearly defeated some travelers. If the height and the narrow rock trails were not bad enough, avalanches and rock slides presented constant danger.

Strategy Tip

Look carefully at the map. What prediction can you make about how difficult it might have been to travel on the Silk Road? Why do you think so?

The Silk Road

From the Pamirs, the caravans inched down to what is now Afghanistan. The traveling there became easier. The caravans took different routes. Some traveled through northern India. Others went to the north, through Samarkand, now called Uzbekistan. The caravans had even more choices of routes as they moved farther west.

Vocabulary Tip

You can use content clues to decode *traverse*. The traveler Marco Polo *traversed* the Silk Road. He wrote about his *journey*. The *trip* took three years. These words tell you that to *traverse* the Silk Road means to "go across" it.

The Adventures of Marco Polo

Perhaps the most famous traveler to **traverse** the Silk Road was Marco Polo. He left Venice in A.D. 1271 and wrote a detailed account of his 5,600-mile (9,010 km) journey. It took Marco Polo, his father, and his uncle three years to reach China. When they arrived, they found great wealth. Marble and gold, paintings and statues were everywhere. The book they wrote about their 24-year trip through Asia became one of the most well-read books of the time. However, few people believed the tales of Polo's adventures in China.

The glories of the Silk Road dimmed in the 1400s. The rise and fall of governments made the route unsafe. In addition, sailors found a passage from Europe to China that made the hazards of the Silk Road unnecessary.

The Silk Road remains an important part of world history because it connected the cultures of Europe and Asia. This connection fostered an exchange of ideas, of goods, of people, and of languages. The Silk Road marked the beginning of understanding between the two continents.

Look over your PACA notes. Do you need to add any major points or any supporting information? If so, add them to the Predictions column. Then add a star to the small box. When you finish, you should have a good understanding of the selection you just read.

Apply It . . . . To check your understanding of the selection, circle the best answer to each question below.

1. Which of these statements is *not* true?
   a. The Silk Road was an active trade route for about 1,600 years.
   b. Marco Polo's book about China was popular in Europe when it was published.
   c. Takla Makan is a terrifying mountain range.
   d. Silk was worth its weight in gold in ancient Rome.

Test Tip

Question 2 asks you to *predict* an answer. You predict an answer in the same way that you predict what you will read. Think about what you know and what you can find out. Then make a reasonable guess at an answer.

2. You might predict that if Europeans had known the secret of silk making,
   a. China would have been even more popular as the source of silkworms.
   b. fewer traders would have made the dangerous journey on the Silk Road.
   c. the Silk Road's popularity would have stayed the same.
   d. silk would have been less desired in Rome.

3. The word *fostered* in the last paragraph means
   a. helped bring about.
   b. stopped.
   c. pictured.
   d. delayed.

Geography:
The Silk Road

4. Which of these locations is closest to the western end of the Silk Road?
   a. Afghanistan
   b. Changan
   c. the Pamir Mountains
   d. the Takla Makan desert

Test Tip

Notice that each of the answers in question 5 contains two parts. *Both* parts must be correct for the answer to be correct.

5. Fewer people traveled the Silk Road in the 1400s because
   a. the route was unsafe and silk was no longer in demand.
   b. silk was less popular and the route was more dangerous.
   c. the route was unsafe and more dangerous.
   d. the route was unsafe and sailors had found an ocean passage from China to Europe.

Use the lines below to write your answers for numbers 6 and 7. Use your PACA chart and the map to help you.

6. Write a description of the Silk Road, including the major stops on the route.

   The Silk Road begins in China in Changan. It goes through 500 miles of fertile land to
   Dunhuang and then 900 miles across the Tarim Basin and the Takla Makan desert.
   From there the road crosses the Pamir Mountains to Afghanistan, where the road
   divides into routes through India, Samarkind (Uzbekistan), and other places.

7. How do you think trade might help cultures understand one another?

   Sample answer: Trade might help connect cultures by making people more
   familiar with each others' ideas, goods, people, and languages.

U.S. History:
Lesson 15 Tragedy at Kent State

Understand It...... During the mid-1960s and early 1970s, students demonstrated against U.S. involvement in the Vietnam War. Use what you know about the protests and the information you see when you preview as you read. The PACA strategy can also help you understand this article.

Try It.............. First, preview the article. Then, on a separate sheet of paper, draw a PACA chart like the one shown below. Write some predictions in the Predictions column. After you read, put check marks next to the predictions that you confirm. Add and star information you did not predict. Add the information that supports your predictions in the Support column.

Strategy Tip

Look at the title and the subheadings. What questions do they raise in your mind? *How* and *why* questions are especially important to ask about this article.

Predictions	Support

Vocabulary Tip

Antiwar begins with the prefix *anti-*, which means "against." So *antiwar* means "against war." Both *distrusted* and *disliked* begin with the prefix *dis-*, which means "not." So *distrusted* means "not trusted" and *disliked* means "not liked."

Tragedy at Kent State

When members of the Ohio National Guard shot four college students at Kent State University, in Kent, Ohio, the country went into shock. The **antiwar** protests against U.S. involvement in the Vietnam War had been bitter. Those who believed in the war **distrusted** and **disliked** the protesters. However, most people opposed the killings.

Beginnings of the Protests

The United States officially became involved in the Vietnam War in 1964. The U.S. government feared that the Communists fighting a civil war in Vietnam would win. Officials felt that would lead to more communism in Southeast Asia. Gradually, U.S. troops entered the fight. By 1965, President Lyndon Johnson was ordering large numbers of U.S. soldiers to Vietnam. By late 1968, student protests had become common.

The Events in May

Antiwar protests at Kent State began after President Richard Nixon announced, on April 30, 1970, that the war was expanding. Activists hit the streets May 1. That evening, violence broke out near Kent State. Police broke up the trouble. The mayor of Kent declared a state of emergency. The governor sent in the Ohio National Guard. (The National Guard in each state keeps order in emergencies.)

On the next night, May 2, more than 1,000 students gathered to protest. The ROTC building, where students trained for military service, was set on fire. Within hours, 900 national guard troops moved onto the campus.

The next day was Sunday. Guards armed with tear gas and rifles stood on the campus. Fearing violence, they ordered an end to a student rally. When some students refused to leave, some guards fired tear gas into the crowd.

At noon on Monday, May 4, about 2,000 people had gathered in the center of campus to take part in a protest. A university police officer with three guards ordered the crowd to break up. The students threw rocks. The guards answered with tear gas.

At that point, many students left. Others kept shouting at the guards. Then, about 100 guards formed a line. The students retreated behind a building. The guards who followed found themselves facing a fence. Students started throwing rocks.

Moments later, about 28 guards turned toward the students. Most of the students were less than 100 yards away. The guards began shooting. The gunfire lasted about 13 seconds. Some soldiers shot into the air. Others aimed at the students.

Four students were killed when National Guard troops fired at antiwar demonstrators at Kent State University.

The students screamed and scattered. Thirteen students fell to the ground. Four were dead. Among the students, shock turned to anger. More than 200 refused to leave the area. The president of the university ordered the school to be closed.

Across the nation, more than 200 colleges shut down. However, not everyone agreed about the shootings. Some blamed the guards. Others blamed the students.

After the Tragedy

People disagreed about who was at fault for the killings. A presidential commission reported that the shootings were not necessary. An Ohio grand jury found the guards not guilty. Charges were dropped against 24 students and a professor for inciting a riot.

Twenty years after the deaths at Kent State, the university built a memorial. On a plaque nearby are the names of the dead and injured students. Near the memorial, 58,175 daffodils bloom every spring. They represent the 58,175 American soldiers who died in Vietnam.

After you finish reading the selection, review your PACA chart. Write check marks in the small box of predictions that were correct. Add main points that you did not predict to the Predictions column. Then add a star to the small box. Be sure that you add information to the Support column.

Apply It. . . . . To check your understanding of the article, circle the best answer to each question below.

1. The main idea of this article is
   a. to tell why the Vietnam War divided the people of the United States.
   b. to show that the National Guard was to blame for the deaths at Kent State.
   c. to argue that no one was to blame for the deaths at Kent State.
   (d.) to explain what happened when the students were killed at Kent State.

2. Just before the National Guard fired on the students,
   a. the guards warned they would shoot.
   (b.) the students threw rocks at the guards.
   c. the president of Kent State tried to calm the situation.
   d. the students yelled at the guards.

3. In the second paragraph from the end, *inciting* means
   a. setting on fire.
   b. ending.
   c. being involved with.
   (d.) causing.

4. The protests against the Vietnam War grew stronger when
   a. the draft of students began.
   b. the students felt they were succeeding in stopping the war.
   (c.) President Nixon expanded the war.
   d. the National Guard was sent in.

Use the lines below to write your answers for numbers 5 and 6. You can use your PACA chart to help you.

5. Summarize the events at Kent State that led to the shootings.

   Violence broke out during antiwar protests. The governor called in the National Guard
   to break up the protests. At a student rally, students were asked to leave. When they
   refused, the shooting began. Thirteen students were hit, four were killed.

Test Tip

When you look for *bias*, you look for words that try to persuade the reader to agree with the writer's opinion. If a reading is *biased*, it favors one side over the other.

6. Do you think the writer of this piece showed *bias*? Give examples from the article to support your answer.

   Sample answer: The writer does not show bias; the article presents both sides of the
   generation gap, explains how the students made the situation worse, and then reports
   what the soldiers did.

Lesson 15   **83**

Lesson 16

Geography:
Journey Down the Unknown River

Understand It...... This article is about the exploration of the Colorado River. The PACA strategy can help you learn more about traveling along this river in the 1800s. Use the map to help you make predictions about this selection.

Try It.............. Draw a PACA chart like the one below. Then preview the article. Look at the subheadings, the first and last paragraphs, and the topic sentences. Be sure to look at the map. Since you will be reading a geography selection about a river journey, you can predict that some information will be about landforms and bodies of water.

After you preview the article, write your predictions in the Predictions column of your PACA chart. Remember to make a check mark next to each prediction that proved to be correct. When you see important information you did not predict, write that. Make a star next to these points. In the Support column, write the evidence that confirms or supports each prediction.

Predictions	Support

Journey Down the Unknown River

On maps, the only label was "unexplored." About 300 miles wide and 500 miles long, the entire Colorado Plateau region in Utah and Arizona was a mystery to mapmakers. The Colorado River flowed through it and no one had traveled the length of the river and survived. In 1869, John Wesley Powell set out to learn more about the mighty Colorado.

Powell, although inexperienced, had long wanted to be the first to explore the Grand Canyon by boat. In 1869, Powell talked his wartime friend, President Ulysses S. Grant, into allowing Powell and his crew to take food from government posts in the West. Armed with the presidential order for food, Powell and his crew began their journey.

Powell packed his wooden boats tightly. He thought the group might be on the river ten months. Each of the three large boats carried 2,000 pounds of supplies. A smaller fourth boat would serve as a scout boat. The nine-member crew was eager but apprehensive. No one knew whether the explorers would be able to find a way out once they were on the river in the Grand Canyon. People had told fearful tales of the Grand Canyon and the river that ran through it. They spoke of

Strategy Tip
Since you are looking for information to add to your Predictions column, you may want to change your reading speed. The more you need to understand, the slower you should read.

thundering waterfalls, whirlpools that plunged people to their deaths, and impossible rapids.

Strategy Tip

When you preview and look at a map, a photograph, or an illustration, make sure to read the caption, too. Captions sometimes point to important ideas in an article.

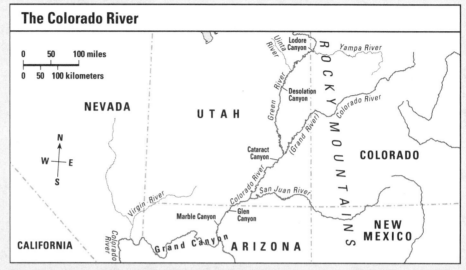

The Colorado River

Powell's crew traveled 240 miles down the Colorado River.

Vocabulary Tip

The word *uneventfully* has several parts. It has a base word, *event*; a prefix, *un-*, which means "not"; and a suffix, *-fully*, which means "full of." Put the word parts together to define the word: "not full of events," or "smoothly."

On the River

The expedition left on May 24, 1869, from Green River, Colorado. The swift current swept the boats downstream. For 60 miles, the boats traveled swiftly but **uneventfully**. There were no high canyons and no rapids.

At the first sight of rapids, the party stopped and spent three days measuring the height of the cliffs and taking scientific notes. Then the boats plunged into what Powell named Horseshoe Canyon. The first rapid scared them and then thrilled them as they ran it successfully.

The walls of the canyon got steeper by the minute. The river narrowed, and the rapids became more violent. Because the rapids could be frightening, the men preferred running them with a slower but safer plan. The boats were first unloaded, attached to a rope, and led gently over the falls or the rapid by the crew. Then the crew carried the tons of supplies around to meet the boat.

After going through a fierce rapid the crew named the Canyon of Lodore, the crew of one of the boats struggled to make shore. Horrified, the rest of the men watched as the boat hurtled over a steep fall and then struck a boulder. The men were flung out and swept helplessly down the river. The boat smashed on the rocks below. The men were rescued, but all the food on the boat, as well as the equipment, was lost.

The next misfortune occurred when the crew built a cooking fire too close to some willow trees, and the fire burned the crew's camping spot. After that, life was calm for a time. On June 18, the crew members

Lesson 16 **85**

Geography:
Journey Down the Unknown River

Strategy Tip

When you review your chart, remember to cross out predictions that were not correct.

floated past the spot where the Yampa River flows into the Green River, and the water is swift and smooth. They traveled through the wide, slow section of the Green where the Uinta River runs. The canyon walls became higher and higher, the rock more and more barren. At one point, rapids pitched several men out of their boat. With the help of two other men, Powell managed to save himself and the boat.

At the stretch of the river called Desolation Canyon, the crew found one rapid after another. Then came 18 miles of small rapids made up of swift, sparkling water that the men enjoyed running. At the site of what is now Green River, Utah, they passed one of the few known crossings of the river. On the afternoon of July 16, they met the Grand River.

On the Grand and the Colorado

On July 21, the group members floated into the Colorado River. Although the Colorado had gentle stretches, it also had terrifying rapids. Some were in canyons too narrow to walk the supplies around. More than once, they shot down a blind waterfall, sure they were plunging to their deaths. They named that stretch of rapids Cataract Canyon.

The next challenge was Marble Canyon, one of the most dangerous stretches of the river. The river squeezed between the flinty rocks, and the rapids pounded the boats. The walls grew higher and higher, reaching 3,000 feet up to the canyon rim. Powell demanded they spend two days repairing the boats.

Powell feared the stretch ahead. "We have an unknown distance yet to run; an unknown river yet to explore," he wrote. In reality, 217 miles lay ahead, and then calm water. Before the easy water, though, lay a terrible stretch of rapids.

On August 27, with about five days worth of food left, the party came upon what they thought of as the most dangerous rapid yet. One man called it "a hell of foam." Powell climbed the canyon walls to take a look at the rapid. He could see no way to walk around it. It was, one man wrote, "the darkest day of the trip."

After three crew members abandoned the trip, the rest of the crew got back on the river, straining to beat the furious water. They went down the falls, broke into the waves, and rowed desperately for shore. Several rapids later, the boats floated into calm water. When they reached the mouth of the Virgin River on August 30, the men saw a group of Native Americans fishing. The men had made it. They were the first to travel through the Grand Canyon by boat.

Look at your PACA notes. Did you include all the main points and supporting information? If not, do so. Then add a star to the small box in the Predictions column. When you finish, you should have a good understanding of the selection you just read.

Apply It. . . . . To check your understanding of the article, circle the best answer to each question below.

1. Which of these hardships did Powell and his crew face on their trip?
   a. angry landowners
   b. dangerous rapids
   c. poorly built boats
   d. flash floods

2. You can infer that Powell wanted to run the river because
   a. he was adventurous.
   b. he wanted exciting objects for his museum.
   c. he wanted the government to take notice of his talents.
   d. he wanted to prove to President Grant that he could do it.

3. "The nine-member crew was eager but apprehensive. . . . People had told fearful tales of the Grand Canyon. . . ." In this passage, *apprehensive* means
   a. busy.
   b. fearful.
   c. prepared.
   d. unwilling.

4. John Wesley Powell can best be described as
   a. foolish and brave.
   b. determined and brave.
   c. cautious and scientific.
   d. independent and commanding.

Test Tip

When a test question asks you to *infer* an answer, think about what you have read. Which of these choices seems most logical?

5. You can infer that the last major rapid the men faced
   a. was more frightening because they were homesick.
   b. could have been walked around if the men had been stronger.
   c. was so dangerous because the boats were damaged.
   d. looked more dangerous because the men were exhausted.

Use the lines below to write your answers for numbers 6 and 7. Use your PACA notes to help you.

6. Suppose that you are Powell. Explain to President Grant why he should support your trip.

   Students may write that if they were Powell, they would want Grant's support because the adventure had never been successfully completed. They may also note Powell's determination and bravery.

7. What might you have found most difficult about the trip?

   Students may feel that the dangerous rapids might be the most difficult problem.

Unit 4 Review: **PACA**

In this unit, you have practiced using the PACA reading strategy. Use this strategy when you read the selection below. Use a separate sheet of paper to draw a chart, take notes, and summarize what you learn.

Hint

Remember that all reading strategies have activities for before, during, and after reading. To review these steps, look at the inside back cover of this book.

Fall of the Berlin Wall

It was November 9, 1989. A man paused and then swung his hammer. Chunks of concrete came raining down. The crowd cheered. It was yet another blow at one of the most hated symbols in Europe: the Berlin Wall.

That night, the concrete and barbed-wire divider fell between East Berlin and West Berlin. A hated symbol of the Cold War after World War II became part of history.

The wall went up after Germany lost World War II. At the end of the war, Berlin was surrounded by the Soviets, who had fought on the side of the Allies against Germany. In 1949, the area officially became East Germany. As a result, Berlin was divided into East Berlin, which was controlled by the Soviets, and West Berlin, which was controlled by the French, British, and Americans.

Those in East Berlin soon realized that the economic conditions in their Communist part of the city were worse than the conditions in thriving West Berlin. East Germans began leaving for the West. In 1961, the wall went up to keep the East Germans from escaping to the capitalist West.

The wall was 12 feet high and 103 miles long, with deep ditches along the eastern side. There were two closely guarded openings in the wall, and East German soldiers patrolled them. The wall became a symbol of the tension between East and West and between communism and democracy. Yet, some people still managed to escape. More than 170 died, 59 as victims of bullets from East German guards.

In the late 1980s, communism began to fall apart in Eastern Europe. Hungary and Poland began economic programs that leaned away from communism. In the summer of 1989, the wall lost its power when Hungary began allowing East Germans to pass through Hungary on their way to nations such as West Germany.

Meanwhile, the East German government was on the edge of collapse. Soon citizens began taking down the wall. In 1990, the two

Germanys reunited as the Federal Republic of Germany.

While the joining of the two halves of Germany was significant, the more emotional event was the destruction of the wall. West Berliners threw flowers at their long-lost fellow residents. Families that had been separated reunited. Thousands streamed through the broken concrete. The cold war was over.

Use your PACA chart to help you answer the questions below.

1. Which is the best explanation of why the Berlin Wall was built?
   a. The Soviets built it to keep people from leaving Germany.
   b. East Germany built it to keep East Germans from leaving the country.
   c. East Germany built it to keep West Germany from attacking.
   d. West Germany built it to keep East Germans from coming to West Germany.

2. Which describes the correct order in which events occurred?
   a. Berlin was divided, the wall fell, East and West Germany reunited.
   b. The Berlin Wall was built, Berlin was divided into sectors, the two Berlins were reunited.
   c. The wall was built, the wall fell, many East Germans escaped into West Germany.
   d. East Germans escaped into West Germany, the two Germanys were reunited, the wall fell.

3. "While the joining of the two halves of Germany was significant, the more emotional event was the destruction of the wall." In this sentence, significant means
   a. easy.
   b. difficult.
   c. important.
   d. unimportant.

4. Explain why residents of East Germany felt safe destroying the wall in November of 1989.

   By 1989, communism was falling in Eastern Europe. Hungary began allowing East Germans to pass through Hungary on their way to West Germany. Also, the German government was collapsing.

5. Describe the effects of the Berlin Wall on the residents of East and West Berlin.

   East Berlin (communism) suffered from financial turmoil while West Berlin (democracy) thrived. The wall was intended to keep East Germans from escaping. As a result, families were separated.

Vocabulary Strategies

Everyone finds unfamiliar words while reading. People approach these new words in many different ways. In some readings, you can tell a word's meaning from the context. In this section, you will learn some new methods for understanding vocabulary words. You may also be reviewing methods you already know.

Using Word Maps to Understand Unknown Words

When you know a word is critical to understanding a selection, create a word map to help you understand its meaning. For example, you may be reading a selection about animals titled *Animal Migration*. If you do not know what the word *migration* means, you need to find out to understand the selection. Your first step may be to preview the selection. As you preview, you collect information about the word. Here is what a word map about migration might look like:

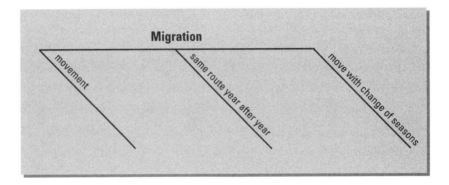

The reader who made this word map now has some ideas about migration. She knows that it involves movement, that it happens with a change in seasons, and that animals migrate using the same route. Now the reader can read the selection with more understanding.

In these lessons, you will learn more methods to help you understand the words you read.

Exercise 1   Words with Multiple Meanings

Understand It......   A word may appear in different subject areas and have a different meaning in each one. Here are two ways to help you understand words with multiple, or several, meanings.

- **Choose from among the meanings you know.** You may know that the word *cell* can mean two things. A *cell* can be a basic unit of living matter. A *cell* can also be a small room in a prison. When you see a word that you know has more than one meaning, think about what you are reading. Which meaning would fit better in the subject you are reading about?

- **Pause if the word you know doesn't make sense.** For example, you may know one meaning of the word *legend*. A *legend* can be a story that is handed down through the years by a people. But read this sentence:

> Look at the map **legend** to find the symbol for camping spots.

The meaning in that sentence is different from the one you may know. If you find a word you think you know, but that word doesn't make sense, look it up. That word probably has multiple meanings.

Below are two passages that use the same words in different ways. Read both passages. Then look at the words in bold type. Use the suggestions above to understand what the words mean in each passage.

Example 1
I wanted to make a circle graph. I wanted to show the different amounts of fruits the country imports. I divided the circle into six **sectors**. Each sector showed how much of one fruit the country imported. The sector for apples was the largest. The country imports more apples than any other fruit. I plan to make graphs now whenever I can. It takes some **intelligence** to make them, but it is worth it.

Example 2
They were the fly boys. According to one officer, these war pilots were not shy.

"Once, they had orders to fly to a new **sector**." No one had flown there before. The flyers wouldn't do it until they had better **intelligence**," the officer said.

Try It..............   To check your understanding of the vocabulary words, circle the best answer to each question below.

1. In Example 1, the word *sectors* means
   a. parts.
   b. angles.
   c. circles.
   d. lines.

Exercise 1 **91**

Words with Multiple Meanings

2. Which of these is the best word for *intelligence* in Example 2?
   a. information
   b. success
   c. understanding
   d. mental ability

3. Which of the following statements is *false*?
   a. In Example 1, *sector* is another word for "section."
   b. The meaning of *intelligence* is the same in both examples.
   c. In Example 2, *sector* means a "specific area."
   d. In Example 1, *intelligence* means "mental ability."

More words with multiple meanings: Sometimes words that we use every day have different meanings in different content areas. Read the two definitions for each word below. Then choose a word from the list that fits both definitions. Write the word on the line.

date	bed	bark	yard	cape

4. _____ cape _____
   Common use: a sleeveless garment worn around the shoulders
   Geography: a piece of land extending into the water

5. _____ date _____
   Common use: the fruit of one type of palm tree
   History: the exact point in time at which an event takes place

6. _____ yard _____
   Common use: the ground around or next to a house or other building
   Mathematics: a measure of length

7. _____ bark _____
   Common use: the short, sharp noise made by dogs
   Science: the outer covering of a tree

8. _____ bed _____
   Common use: a piece of furniture on which to sleep
   Geography: the bottom of a river

Exercise 2   Context Clues: Part I

Understand It...... One of the ways active readers figure out the meaning of words they do not know is by using context clues. They can help you understand what a word means.

- **Look at the words around the word you do not know.** These words can help you define the new word.

- **Look for all the times the word is used.** Sometimes a word you don't know is repeated or restated. Look at the places the word is used for clues.

Read the paragraph. Use context clues to understand the words in bold type.

> Food chains are chains of living things that depend on each other. **Herbivores** are animals that eat plants. A bird that eats seeds is an example of an **herbivore**. Meat-eaters, or **carnivores**, are at the top of the food chain. A wolf is one example of a **carnivore**. **Carnivores** eat **herbivores**. Some **carnivores** eat other **carnivores**, too.

Try It.............. To check your understanding of the vocabulary entries, circle the best answer to each question below.

1. What is the best description of *carnivore*?
   a. a plant-eating animal
   b. an animal-eating animal
   c. an herbivore
   d. an animal eaten by bacteria and fungi

2. Which of these statements is correct?
   a. An herbivore is a plant that gets its food from the sun.
   b. An herbivore is an animal that eats only animals.
   c. An herbivore is an animal that eats plants and animals.
   d. An herbivore is an animal that eats only plants.

Use context clues to figure out the meaning of the term in bold type. Write a definition for that term in the space provided.

3. While sales at the Lakeland Corporation have nearly tripled, sales at the Regis Corporation are **plummeting**.
   declining, going down _____

   _____

4. The contract negotiations are becoming increasingly **partisan**; neither management nor the labor union is willing to give in.
   divided _____

   _____

Exercise 3 Context Clues: Part II

Understand It....... Sometimes writers make it easy for readers to understand difficult words. They add definitions, restatements, or synonyms. Other times authors use examples that show the word's meaning, or compare or contrast the word to other known words. Once you know these tools, you may find yourself understanding more of what you read. Here are some of those tools:

- **Definitions, restatements, and synonyms.** If authors think a word may be difficult, often they will help their readers by defining the word right there. They may also restate the meaning of the word or show the meaning through a synonym. Here is an example of each:

  > *Definition:* She studied **biology**, which is the study of living things.
  >
  > *Restatement:* The **goslings**, those fuzzy baby geese, waddled after their mother.
  >
  > *Synonym:* Dan was feeling so **distressed**, so upset, by the grade he got, that he refused to come to the party.

- **Meaning through example.** Sometimes authors use an example to show the meaning of a word in action. Examples may be shown by words such as *for instance, for example,* and *such as.* The following sentence shows you how it works:

  > The scientist found many basic **raw materials**, such as minerals, while in the field collecting samples.

- **Comparisons and contrasts.** A sentence may include a comparison that shows how the unknown word is like another word. The words *like, as,* and *similar to* may signal this. A contrast shows how a word is unlike another word. Look for words such as *but, however, instead, on the contrary,* and *on the other hand* in contrasts. For example:

  > *Comparison:* Carol was **as** congenial as the friendliest person I know.
  >
  > *Contrast:* Little Danny was **sorrowful,** but his new toy made him happy.

Try It.............. Read the following sentences.

> Production at the Dallas division of the Lakeland Corporation is completely **automated.** However, production at the Columbus division is done by hand.

1. Which words act as a signal and help you figure out the meaning of the word *automated?*

by hand

2. What does the word *automated* mean?

done by machines

Read the paragraphs below. Use context tools to help you understand the meaning of the words in bold type. Then answer the questions below.

> **Impeachment** is a charge against a high official for a crime. It is not common in the United States. President Andrew Johnson was **impeached** after the Civil War. The Senate held a trial. Johnson had **vetoed** many bills instead of signing them as laws. He and Congress fought. Johnson wanted to make it easier for Southern states to rejoin the country, but Congress did not.
>
> Finally, the Senate held the trial. Although each side offered evidence, Johnson was not convicted. Instead, he was **acquitted** of the charges against him. He served out his term in office.

To check your understanding of the vocabulary entries, circle the best answer to each question below.

3. Impeachment is
   a. a trial during which a high official is tried.
   (b.) a charge against a high official.
   c. the conviction of an official for high crimes.
   d. the process of trying a high official for a crime.

4. Which is the best definition for the word *veto?*
   a. to sign a bill into law
   b. to vote for a law
   c. to argue against a bill that will be made into a law
   (d.) to reject a bill and not allow it to become a law

5. If you are *acquitted* of a crime, you
   (a.) are not convicted.
   b. must go to trial.
   c. cannot be convicted of a crime.
   d. are convicted.

Exercise 4　Signal Words

You often see words in directions. They tell you in what order to do things and allow you to follow a reading selection more easily. Here are some of those words:

- **Words that give you steps.** You may often see these words when you are reading a science experiment. You will see them in writing that describes a process. You also will see them when you are following directions. If you put together a bike, for example, you may see a series of steps that you should take.

Some of these words are number words, such as *first*, *second*, and *last*. Others help you keep track of the order in which you should do something, such as *before* and *then*. Here is an example of how you might see these words:

> **First**, put the sugar and the water in the pan. **Second**, turn up the heat to high. **Next**, cook until the mixture bubbles. **Finally**, let it cool.

- **Words that tell you what is coming next.** Often writers will tell you what is coming next by using these signal words. You may remember seeing words such as *therefore* or *in conclusion*. These words will give you clues to what the writer is doing. Notice the signal words in the sentences below.

> Let me restate this point. No one is sure what this drug will do. **Therefore**, I will not approve it. **In conclusion**, I must say that no one should ever take this unsafe drug.

When you see the words *in conclusion*, you know the writer is signaling that he or she is reviewing, or summing up, the selection.

Read the paragraphs below. Use signal words to help you understand how the words in bold type are used. Then answer the questions below.

> If you plan to do this experiment, follow these steps. **First**, gather all of your materials. **Second**, clean your equipment well. **Last**, make sure all of your equipment is working. If you do all these things in this order, you will have done all you can to make sure your experiment will work.
>
> **In conclusion**, let me end my paper by summarizing for you the most important conclusions of my research. **First**, there is not enough information available to say if the horned bat will ever return. Even

though we have an idea that the bat has found other places to live, we do not know that for certain. **Second**, there are no plans to create a new habitat near here. **Finally**, and **most important**, there is no money to continue studying this topic. I am afraid the horned bats have to survive on their own.

Try It. . . . . To check your understanding of the signal words, circle the best answer to each question below.

1. Which of these steps comes last?
   a. preparing for the experiment
   (b.) making sure the equipment is working
   c. cleaning the equipment well
   d. getting together all materials

2. What is the author signaling when she writes *in conclusion*?
   (a.) that she is briefly reviewing her findings
   b. that she is at the beginning of her arguments
   c. that this is the research that took the most time
   d. that these are the steps that listeners should follow

3. What is the *most important* conclusion of the scientist writing the second paragraph?
   a. Horned bats are extinct.
   (b.) There is no money left for research on the bats.
   c. No one can say if the horned bats will return.
   d. There are no new habitats for the horned bats.

4. Read the following list. Number the entries in time order.
   __2__ Second, listen for a dial tone.
   __4__ Finally, tell the dispatcher where the fire is.
   __1__ First, pick up the phone.
   __3__ After that, dial 911.

5. Number the following sentences in correct order.
   __2__ First, I missed the bus that I take to school.
   __1__ My first day of school was very hectic.
   __5__ Luckily, I found a seat in the back of class, so no one saw me come in late.
   __4__ As a result, I was 15 minutes late.
   __3__ Then I had to wait ten extra minutes so my mom could drive me.

Apply What You Have Learned

Use the strategies you have learned in this book to analyze the following selections. If you need to review the steps of any strategy, look at the inside back cover of this book. Use the Vocabulary Tips to help you with words that may be unfamiliar. Circle any other words that you need to define.

Review 1

World History: The Battle of Belleau Wood

It was June of 1918. World War I was raging in Europe. The Allies had been fighting Germany for four years. U.S. troops had recently entered the war. How could they help their exhausted allies? The Battle of Belleau Wood was important for what it showed about the U.S. troops—to themselves, to their allies in Europe, and to the Germans.

Belleau Wood is a small area in northern France. It was near a highway that led to Paris. The army that controlled the area controlled the highway. Germany had taken it, and the Allies wanted it back.

A Test for the United States

The battle was critical for the United States. The French commander wanted U.S. soldiers to take the places of Allied soldiers who had died. The U.S. commander, General John Pershing, opposed that idea. He wanted his men to fight under a U.S. commander. At Belleau Wood, the United States had a chance to prove its fighting ability. General Pershing wanted to prove his soldiers were more than just fill-ins for the dead and wounded.

The U.S. troops went into a situation deadly enough to frighten any experienced soldier. As they entered the forest, U.S. soldiers met exhausted French soldiers who were leaving. One U.S. soldier wrote, "They looked at us like we were mad. We were walking into a **sector** that they had given up as lost. The French kept motioning with their hands, go back, go back." Fresh and eager to show their abilities, the U.S. troops had no thought of retreating. They had reached their proving ground.

The Germans had a great advantage. Belleau Wood was only one mile square. Huge boulders were everywhere. These boulders and the wood's thick trees gave the German machine guns excellent cover. In addition, the Germans had had plenty of time to hide themselves.

Vocabulary Tip

The word *sector* may remind you of another word you know: *section*. Use this clue to help you define *sector*.

The Terrible Battle

The battle began on June 6, 1918. U.S. troops experienced heavy losses. They went into the wood and died one after another as the German machine gunners mowed them down. "They leaped forward and fell in droves," one historian wrote. The soldiers pressed on. For 20 days, the battle raged. Guns roared 24 hours a day. Water was scarce, and there was no chance to cook food. The U.S. soldiers ate raw bacon and potatoes they dug from the ground.

Slowly, yard by yard, the U.S. troops gained ground. They crawled over the bodies of their dead friends. They faced machine-gun fire again and again. On June 25, the United States took the wood.

However, the victory was **bittersweet**. More than half of the U.S. soldiers sent into Belleau Wood—1,087 soldiers—had been killed or badly injured. Was it worth it? Some said no. The tiny wood had cost too many lives.

Others, though, looked at what the victory meant to both sides. The Europeans no longer had any doubt about the ability of the U.S. troops. They had no doubt about their spirit, either. U.S. soldiers were ready to fight.

If the U.S. determination impressed the Allies, it terrified the Germans. One German soldier commented that U.S. soldiers were "crazy fellows, who fight like devils."

In war, attitude can matter. So can appearances. When U.S. troops went into Belleau Wood, they proved they were willing to take huge risks—and huge losses—to win. This gave new strength to their European allies. Just as important, U.S. soldiers made the Germans afraid. In war, feelings do count. One French officer said, "You Americans are our hope, our strength, our life."

Vocabulary Tip

The word *bittersweet* is a compound word. It is made up of two smaller words. What are those words? How do the words work together to make another word?

New York City was the first place many immigrants saw when they reached the United States. It is not surprising that many stayed there. Hell's Kitchen is a neighborhood in the middle of Manhattan, a part of New York City. This history of Hell's Kitchen tells the story of some of these immigrants.

There are many theories about how this area of New York City got its nickname. Some say it was because the area was so poor and there was so much violence. Others point out that the nickname was 19th-century slang for any poor area. Still others think one of the tenement houses was given the name. It stuck to the entire area because it fit.

Of course, bad conditions were common for immigrant groups wherever they settled in the large cities of the United States. Often, immigrants arrived with little money and few ideas about how to get work. They understood little about their new country, and many spoke little English. They had few choices of jobs. They also knew few people.

That explains why so many immigrants stayed together and settled in the poorest neighborhoods. A neighborhood might be filthy and overcrowded. It might be dangerous. However, people spoke the same language and followed the same customs. Newcomers could even find some foods from home.

From Flowers to Filth

According to *Virgil: The Guide to Hell's Kitchen,* this is a brief history of Hell's Kitchen and its residents. In 1803, the very wealthy businessman John Jacob Astor bought the area. At the time, it was a farm called the "Vale of Flowers." In 1803, that name fit.

In 1854, the first school was built there. It was a quiet country school. The country ways were beginning to fade, however, as New York City grew northward. By the 1860s, there was nothing left of the Vale of Flowers.

After the Dutch farmers left, the next immigrants to settle in the area were Irish and German. They lived in crowded tenement buildings. The living conditions in these tenements were terrible. A state legislature report in 1864 noted that the cattle in the neighborhood lived better than the people did. Lawmakers passed regulations requiring at least one outdoor or indoor toilet for every 20 tenants.

In the early 1860s, the Tenth Avenue Gang ruled. It joined with the Hell's Kitchen Gang in 1868. This violent gang specialized in mugging and robbery. Gang members also demanded **protection money** from local stores.

Vocabulary Tip

Even though you may not know the term *protection money,* you can figure out its meaning. Look at the individual words. Then look at the way they appear in the sentence.

In the 1870s, social activists in New York City began to clean up Hell's Kitchen. An 1881 article in the *The New York Times* listed the problems of the neighborhood. It was filthy. Rats ruled. Smells from the slaughterhouses sickened visitors. The people wore rags. The apartments were small, crowded, and had no heat. Most did not have indoor plumbing.

However, as each immigrant group found its way in the United States, many people in the group moved on. They gained enough knowledge and money to leave the area. They wanted better places to live and better schools.

Italians moved in during the 1920s. Then came Greeks and Poles. Other Eastern Europeans arrived. After World War II, new groups arrived. Puerto Ricans came. African Americans from the South moved to the cities. Many who came to New York City found shelter in Hell's Kitchen.

Hell's Kitchen Changes Again

By the 1950s, the area began to change again. Tenements were torn down. Even so, much of the immigrant **flavor** remained into the 1960s. Lorenzo Carcaterra, author of *Sleepers,* described the Hell's Kitchen of those days as still poor. "It was an area populated by an uneasy blend of Irish, Italian, Puerto Rican, and Eastern European laborers, hard men living hard lives, often by their own design."

In the 1980s, rents rose sharply in New York City. Suddenly, Hell's Kitchen became an affordable place for young professionals to live. Today, some of the first residents remain, mixing with the newcomers. The Hell's Kitchen of gangs and hard living is largely a thing of the past, but its history remains as a short course in immigrant life.

Vocabulary Tip

The word *flavor* is used here in an unusual way. Use what you know about the word to figure out its meaning in this paragraph.

Government: The Rise of Fascism

After World War I, a new system of government arose in Europe. In just a few years, it was widespread. This system—**fascism**—was based on the idea that the state is more important than the individual. Fascist governments are led by a dictator who holds all of the power.

The word *fascism* comes from the Latin word *fasces*. The fasces was an ancient Roman symbol: a bundle of rods tied together around an ax. To fascists, the fasces stood for the power of the state. The name was created by Benito Mussolini, an Italian leader who brought fascism to Italy in the 1920s.

Fascist governments did not exist only in Italy, however. Fascist leaders also came to power in Germany and in several other European countries.

The Beginnings of Fascism

Mussolini's new movement began in Italy after World War I. Although Italy had fought with the Allies, life was hard after the war. People were hungry. Money was scarce. Rebuilding was difficult. Mussolini used the Italians' deep anger about their condition to fuel his takeover.

Italians were desperate for better times. Mussolini promised strong leadership. He said that if he were given power, people's lives would be easier. He also said he would rebuild Italy into a strong nation. Many people saw him as a savior and a father figure. To the landowners and those who ran big businesses, Mussolini promised that there would be no social unrest. He promised success for everyone. All people had to do was forget individual concerns and obey the state. His slogan was "to believe, to obey, to combat."

Mussolini took control of the Italian government in 1922. As a dictator, he had total power. The first thing Mussolini did was to **disband** all other political parties. Then he banned labor unions and outlawed strikes. That made big businesses happy. He also cut wages and forced Italians to stay on the farms and work.

Mussolini saw war as a way to solve the country's problems. You can see that belief in this saying: "Nothing has ever been won in history without bloodshed!" Mussolini believed in war

Benito Mussolini during a political speech at a mass rally

Vocabulary Tip

To find the meaning of *disband*, look at the word's parts. The root word is *band*, and the prefix is *dis-*. To *band together* means "to join." *Dis-* means "not." When you put these word parts together, you find that *to disband* means "to break apart."

for its own sake, however. He thought the military values of obedience and sacrifice were important to Italy's success.

In some ways, fascism did succeed in Italy—for a short time. The trains ran on time. Big businesses and farms did well. Most people suffered, though. They had little to eat. Mussolini dismissed this complaint. He said that because the Italian people were not used to eating much, they felt the pangs of hunger less.

Fascism survived in Italy until World War II. Then Italy joined with two other fascist powers—Germany and Japan—to form an alliance called "the Axis." When the Axis powers lost the war, fascism died in Italy.

Fascism in Germany

In Germany, fascism was called National Socialism. Adolf Hitler took advantage of the same opportunity as Mussolini after World War I. Germany had also lost World War I. The German people were hungry and had trouble rebuilding their country. No one seemed to be able to help.

The Germans saw Hitler as a strong leader who could take control and lead them to prosperity. In German fascism, the idea that the nation was superior also meant that the German "race" was superior. That belief was the basis for the Holocaust.

During the Holocaust, six million Jews were murdered. Other people who did not fit Hitler's idea of the "master race" were also killed. They included people with physical and mental disabilities and people with dark skin.

Fascism After World War II

Since World War II, fascism has not been as popular as it had been between the world wars. Today, the world looks on the governments of Hitler and Mussolini as evil. People remember how these two leaders promised to lead their countries out of a dark period. They also remember how those promises led to an even darker period—of hunger, murder, and the loss of basic individual rights. Even though a government might have some fascist policies, its leaders would not call themselves fascists today.

Sociology:
Levittown, The Birth of the Suburb

World War II was over. Veterans wanted to marry, find jobs, and start families. However, the country was not ready for them. One family understood the needs of these young people. Many people consider that family, the Levitts, the pioneers of **suburbia** in this country.

Congress wanted to provide low-cost housing for war veterans. Many had sacrificed their education and good jobs to help the war effort. Lawmakers helped builders finance the houses they built for veterans. Congress also offered veterans low-cost mortgages to help them buy houses.

The Levitts Build a Town

The Levitts had begun buying potato fields on Long Island, New York, before the war ended. William Levitt thought he could build houses on an assembly line, like cars. One group of workers would put on roofs. Another group would build the framing. Levitt built 2,000 houses in 1947.

The Levitts' community soon became controversial. Many people thanked the Levitts for providing veterans with low-cost housing. Many veterans otherwise would not have been able to rent or buy a house.

Those who hated the place hated it because all the houses looked alike. Others did not like it because the residents looked alike. For many years, the Levitts refused to sell to African Americans.

The veterans who wanted to move in could do so. Almost 5,000 applied for the first 2,000 houses. "Each house had GE appliances, a Bendix washer, and its own big 12-inch Admiral television set," another of the first homeowners said. "To be able to move into a new home with all these new luxury items for no money down was unbelievable."

Levittown Grows

At first, the community was little more than a collection of identical houses. There were very few trees. The houses had no telephones. There were no churches or schools. Most of the residents were about the same age and came from similar backgrounds. Their children grew up together.

Levittown continued to grow. Eventually, about 17,000 houses were built. A few lots were used for parks or pools. There were no schools, however. Levittown's homeowners had to buy the land to build schools.

Levittown: Good or Bad?

Suburbs like Levittown sprang up everywhere. Critics said that they caused traffic jams and led people to leave the cities. Critics also said they kept minority groups out.

Defenders of suburbs saw people who wanted to escape the dirt and crime of the cities. Children played in backyards. People were safe.

By the 1970s and 1980s, few Levittown houses looked like the originals. The people had changed, too. People who had needed one another for everything from baby-sitting to borrowing a lawn mower could afford those things themselves.

Times Change for Levittown

By the late 1970s, few African Americans lived in Levittown. Those who did often felt unwelcome. Also, in the 1950s, most women worked in the home. They depended on one another. That changed as they took jobs outside the home. The era of supporting one another was over.

Today, a Levittown home that originally cost $7,000 sells for about $160,000. Buying a home requires a down payment. The suburb is graying, too. The original residents have retired.

In some ways, though, Levittown remains the American dream. It is a symbol of the belief that people who work hard can succeed. It started the most influential housing trend in the second half of the 20th century. Levittown is still the suburb that started it all.

U.S. History:
A Fever in the Land

It started innocently enough in 1692, with a game of fortune-telling. By the end of this terrible time in U.S. history, 20 people had been killed. After an eight-month ordeal, the terror ended.

The Sin of Telling Fortunes

In 1692, children had little to do in Salem Village, Massachusetts. The society was strictly Puritan. Girls stayed inside during the winter, doing chores and reading the Bible. During that winter, the minister's daughter, Betty Parris, age 9, and her cousin Abigail Williams, age 11, amused themselves by listening to the stories of Tituba, an enslaved woman from the West Indies.

Tituba told the folktales of her native land to the girls and several of their friends. She also taught them fortune-telling games, such as dropping an egg white into a glass of water to foretell the job that a future husband would have.

While playing that game, Betty felt guilty because her strict society did not permit such games. As a result of her guilt, Betty believed that she saw a coffin in the water. She began moaning and writhing on the floor like a snake. Soon, Abigail joined her. Alarmed, their friends called the village doctor, William Griggs. He looked at the girls and offered his diagnosis: witchcraft.

Soon other girls began behaving strangely. They screamed and shouted and refused to say their prayers. Witches had caused this, people thought, and the girls had a duty to name them.

Finally, the girls gave the names of people who fit the Puritans' idea of witches. They named as witches three women who were generally disliked. The women did not belong to well-known families, and they had little money or influence. One was Tituba, the enslaved woman. Another was Sarah Goode, a homeless beggar. The third was Sarah Osborne, who had been accused of witchcraft several years earlier.

The Trials Begin

The women were arrested and questioned by the town judges. The girls who had accused them were also in the room. As the women began to answer the judges' questions, the girls again began writhing on the floor.

After her owner, the Reverend Samuel Parris, beat her, Tituba confessed. She described how she rode through the air on a stick to attend meetings of the witches.

The girls named other witches, accusing even well-respected people in the village. At this time, opinions about Reverend Parris's leadership of the church divided the community. Several people had refused to pay their share of his salary. Salem Village had also separated from Salem

Town seven years earlier. The people of the small farming village felt isolated from their richer, more powerful neighbors.

Puritans of Salem Village were eager to find something to blame for their recent troubles. Smallpox had killed many people in the 1680s and 1690s. Droughts in recent years had meant poor harvests. Those events had not happened by chance, people said; they were the result of witchcraft.

A witchcraft trial in Salem, Massachusetts, in 1692

Accused witches quickly filled the jail. A special court was created to deal with the witchcraft trials. Just a week after being established, the court convicted and hanged the first person accused of being a witch. One judge thought that relying only on the girls for evidence was wrong, so he resigned. Soon, he was accused of witchcraft, too.

The court provided little help. The accused had no lawyers and were considered guilty unless proven innocent. Even more difficult to disprove was **"spectral evidence,"** which meant that a person could be accused of causing harm with his or her spirit. The accused person did not even need to be present because he or she was often already in jail.

Stories from the Trials

Each trial had its own horrors. The girls said the spirit of Sarah Goode's daughter, four-year-old Dorcas, had attacked them as revenge for accusing her mother. Encouraged by the judges, Dorcas told stories of the snake her mother had given her. She said her mother hurt the girls. Dorcas was clearly a witch, too. She joined her mother in jail. Then Sarah Goode was executed for witchcraft.

At first, Giles Corey, who was known for his temper, had believed in witches. He even accused his wife of witchcraft but then took back his testimony. The girls told the court how he had given them fits, pinched them, and plotted to destroy the church. The law said an accused person had three chances to plead. A person who did not answer could not be tried. Corey refused to speak, so the judges had him staked to the ground under a board. The judges ordered that the board be weighted with stones until Corey testified. He refused and was pressed to death.

One way to be accused of witchcraft was to be a member of the lower classes of Salem Village society. Another was to make fun of the girls. John Proctor, who criticized the girls and the trial process, became their target. He was, they said, "a most dreadful wizard." He, his wife,

Vocabulary Tip

This sentence says that with *spectral evidence,* "a person could be accused of causing harm with his or her spirit." What does that tell you about the meaning of *spectral*?

and their two oldest children were all accused. Despite his protests to officials in Boston, Proctor was hanged.

The Madness Slows

In October 1692, four months after the trials began, things began to change. The girls had accused the governor's wife and that went too far. Citizens from nearby communities wrote letters against the trials. Fourteen ministers finally urged an end to the trials. The Reverend Cotton Mather, who had been a believer in witchcraft, changed his mind. "I had rather judge a witch to be an honest woman than judge an honest woman to be a witch," he said. ·

When Mather wrote his protest, 150 suspected witches awaited trial. On October 15, the governor **disbanded** the court. When another court heard the cases, 49 of the 52 accused people were declared innocent. The other three confessed witches were later pardoned.

Twenty people had died, and a community had been torn apart. Finally, the accused returned to their homes. Several years passed before they regained their rights as citizens. In 1711, 22 relatives of those who had been executed asked for money to help pay for the loss of their family members. The court granted them their request.

Vocabulary Tip

Think about the meaning of the prefix *dis*—"the opposite of"—and you can understand the meaning of the word *disbanded.*